10.95

D0847768

The Impersonal Campus

Options for Reorganizing Colleges
to Increase Student Involvement,
Learning, and Development

Virginia B. Smith

Alison R. Bernstein

The Impersonal Campus

 Jossey-Bass Publishers

San Francisco • Washington • London • 1979

THE IMPERSONAL CAMPUS
Options for Reorganizing Colleges to Increase Student Involvement, Learning, and Development
by Virginia B. Smith and Alison R. Bernstein

The Jossey-Bass
Series in Higher Education

Preface

The federal education bureaucracy was the catalyst for this book. Although we taught and worked as administrators in two of the largest higher education systems in the country—the University of California system and the City University of New York (CUNY) —we probably would have never written a volume about alternatives to impersonal education had we not spent four years as part of the biggest education organization in the country—the U.S. Department of Health, Education, and Welfare—employed in one of its smallest units—the Fund for the Improvement of Postsecondary Education. Somehow the Fund managed to build an independent identity and operating style despite the constraints imposed upon it by that massive bureaucracy. The Fund's constant struggle to maintain flexibility, responsiveness, and a sense of purpose and community led us to examine the relationship of an organization's size to its function and we wondered whether similar problems arose for colleges and universities. Had the rapid expansion of many of these institutions in the last two decades created difficulties in determining the appropriate relationship of their size to their educational function?

Preface

Thus we undertook the review that led to *The Impersonal Campus* to answer the question: Is there a clear relationship between size of the enterprise and the learning outcomes that can be expected from that enterprise? Prior to coming to the Fund, one of us (Smith) had witnessed firsthand student disaffection with mass undergraduate education as part of the Berkeley protests in the 1960s. The other of us (Bernstein) joined CUNY in the fall of 1970, the year in which open admissions brought 40,000 freshmen into that system, and began teaching there in a mobile trailer, because Staten Island Community College, built to enroll 2,000 students, was asked overnight to accommodate 9,000. On the basis of these experiences, both of us had formulated some tentative hypotheses about the capacity of massive higher education institutions to educate, not just to award credentials to, their students. Our years at the Fund strengthened our conviction that many policy makers and administrators had bought the bigger-is-better rhetoric without analyzing how large-scale operations can have a negative impact on an educational environment.

In the course of our search for an answer, we were surprised at the lack of research and analyses that addressed the relationship of an institution's size to its educational effectiveness. Economists had evidenced an interest in the size of colleges and universities in relation to financing higher education. Educational psychologists like Alexander Astin and Arthur Chickering, on the basis of broad surveys and investigations of nontraditional academic programs, had drawn certain limited conclusions about the impact of a college environment on student development. But, by and large, the field had not been carefully examined.

Undoubtedly the shortage of definitive conclusions on the question owes much to the methodological problems in attempting to isolate size from other variables that affect learning. In the social sciences this is often the case because it is easy to handle in methodological terms those questions that are often hardly worth asking. As a result, the more significant questions frequently go unanswered and, worse, unexamined.

Partly because of this reluctance to address the issue of appropriate scale for learning directly, we became more interested in bringing together those fragments of research and empirical observation related to the topic. Coupled with our own observations and those of individuals undertaking a variety of postsecondary educational efforts, we were able to analyze the issue in more detail than had previously been attempted.

The first two chapters discuss the historical and economic context that encouraged the growth of large-scale higher education institutions and provide partial explanations for the bigger-is-better phenomenon. Given this context, we have concluded that massive institutions became almost inevitable as educators tried to honor society's commitment to mass higher education. The problem was that few policy makers carefully analyzed the premises underlying the assumption that large-scale institutions provide more benefits than smaller ones. If they had, they probably would have found other ways to accommodate mass numbers besides putting more students into existing institutions.

Chapters Three through Six describe new responses to the size question. Both large universities and small colleges are experimenting with programs to maximize learning opportunities. A few massive institutions are trying to "scale down" their curriculums, while smaller schools are testing consortial arrangements that give greater diversity of course offerings and learning programs without jeopardizing the school's sense of community. As Chapters Five and Six suggest, the effort to seek alternatives to education on a massive scale is especially important if institutions are interested in educating the "new" students—working adults, older students, and persons from diverse cultural backgrounds. All too often, these students are the ones in need of the personal attention a small school can provide. But because of financial limitations, they are forced to attend large, comprehensive community and state colleges.

In the final chapter, we call for action from both the research community and from decision makers. By giving examples of how administrators can look at the relationship of size to function, we hope to put our original question to the test—if not across the board in a massive study, then at least on a case-by-case basis. We call this investigation ACTION/RESEARCH because it requires administrators to perform assessments of the actions they have taken. ACTION/RESEARCH should result in a closer fit between an institution's educational goals and its ability to accomplish them. Thus, when a college catalogue proclaims that students learn critical thinking as undergraduates, administrators should be able to demonstrate that the institution can validate the statement.

We admit that persons looking for the definitive answer to our initial question will be, like us, somewhat frustrated by the results. There is no simple relationship between size and quality. Nevertheless, there is a greater *likelihood* that certain types of learning suffer in a massive institution. There are no sweeping generalizations or overt condemnations emerging from this analysis. Instead, we think it provides a much needed framework for discussion and action. We remain concerned that too many institutions have grown too big to be effective, but we are probably more troubled by the fact that educators have not done enough thinking about how to create an atmosphere in which teaching and learning can best occur, and this lack of reflection has resulted in the massiveness of contemporary higher education. Most disturbing of all to us is the possibility that even less analysis will go into the hard decisions that are being thrust upon administrators and faculty by a new period of fiscal constraint. Budgets are being slashed by formulas that frequently bear little or no resemblance to educational concerns, and such "frills" as student support services appear the most expendable. Yet in larger institutions these "frills" may be the only structural mechanisms for counteracting a student's sense of alienation and encouraging self-directed learning.

When we began this book, we believed that administrators would be our primary audience. After all, they were the ones ultimately responsible for the decisions that determined the shape and size of educational programs. As we delved deeper into the subject, we discovered other audiences we wanted to reach—state legislators, who often dictate the terms under which campuses must operate, and our fellow education policy makers in Washington,

Preface

who by their funding patterns reward quantity, not quality, in assessing academic institutions. When we completed the manuscript, we realized that it also might prove valuable to faculty and students concerned about giving and getting a decent education. They may find some clues here that explain why college has become for so many a disappointing and intellectually empty experience.

We are clearly indebted to those rare researchers who have been interested in this question and to those who preceded us in efforts to pull together research on the subject, particularly Donald J. Reichard, whose articles on campus size were very helpful. Although we owe a great deal to the writers and researchers whose work helped us to understand the complexity of the question, this book has benefited primarily from those individuals who are actively pursuing the answers by implementing new programs. Unfortunately, many have not written about their efforts, but they generously gave what little time they had to enlighten us about education in massive institutions and how to improve it. We want to single out our colleagues at the Fund, who are asking the right questions and supporting the kinds of projects that may bring us closer to some answers. We especially thank the project directors whose programs are discussed in the following pages. Their willingness to try alternative approaches puts them on the firing line every day, and we hope this book will help them justify their efforts. Whereas we have written about the problem, they are attempting to solve it. Finally, we want to dedicate this work to one colleague in particular, the late Mina Shaughnessy, whose constant encouragement and suggestions at an early stage of its development proved invaluable. Her untimely death has been a loss to all persons interested in improving higher education.

March, 1979   VIRGINIA B. SMITH
                                                 Poughkeepsie, New York

                                                 ALISON R. BERNSTEIN
                                                 Washington, D.C.

xiii

Contents

Contents

The Authors

VIRGINIA B. SMITH is president of Vassar College in Poughkeepsie, New York. Smith was born in Seattle, Washington. She was awarded the B.A. degree (1944) and the M.A. degree in economics (1950) from the University of Washington, and she took her J.D. degree from the University of Washington's Law School (1946). She taught at the University of Puget Sound (1946–1947) and at Seattle Pacific College (1948–1952), after which she joined the staff of the Institute for Industrial Relations, University of California, Berkeley (1951–1956). In 1958, Smith joined University of California president Clark Kerr's staff where she held a variety of administrative posts, including assistant vice-president of the University of California system.

The Authors

In 1967, Smith went to work for the Carnegie Commission on Higher Education, eventually serving as associate director. In this capacity she had staff responsibility on several reports including *Quality and Equality, City and Campus, Campus and Capitol,* and *Institutional Aid.* In 1973 she became the first director of the Department of Health, Education, and Welfare's (HEW) newly created Fund for the Improvement of Postsecondary Education (FIPSE), and since September 1977 she has been president at Vassar.

As a Fulbright Fellow, Smith studied adult and trade union education in Great Britain, and she recently was named one of forty-four outstanding leaders in higher education.

Smith was admitted to the State Bars of California and Washington and for a number of years practiced law in San Francisco.

ALISON R. BERNSTEIN is a program officer at the Fund for the Improvement of Postsecondary Education, HEW, Washington, D.C.

Bernstein was born in New York City in 1947; she was awarded the B.A. degree in history from Vassar College (1969), and the M.A. degree in history from Columbia University (1970), where she is also completing her Ph.D. degree in twentieth century American history. She began her teaching career as an instructor in history at Staten Island Community College of the City University of New York (1970–1973). While there she directed a special three-year Adult Degree Program and served as assistant to the president. Bernstein joined the staff of FIPSE in 1974.

In 1969 Bernstein was named the first "Young Trustee" in Vassar's history and also received a Danforth fellowship for graduate study. Since then she has served on the Danforth Foundation Advisory Board and has published several articles on higher education, the history of women's education, and open admissions in *Change,* the University of Chicago's *School Review, The Chronicle of Higher Education,* and *Signs: A Journal of Women in Culture and Society.*

The Impersonal Campus

Options for Reorganizing Colleges to Increase Student Involvement, Learning, and Development

CHAPTER ONE

Myths of Bigger Is Better

Americans have tended to believe that anything bigger is bound to be better and worth their attention, whether it is a building, a social organization, an industry, or their own government. Regardless of the task to be performed, they have acted as if it could probably be done better by enlarging the institution or organization performing it. But is bigger really better? An increasing number of voices are being raised against this proposition. One eloquent spokesman, the late British economist E. F. Schumacher, warned in *Small Is Beautiful* (1973, p. 38) that the modern world suffers from an almost "universal idolatry of giantism." Apparently the disease is not confined to our shores.

We can catch a glimpse of what can happen when something becomes too large by considering these lines from poet John

The Impersonal Campus

Ciardi (1964, p. 3): "Some rule of birds kills off the song / in any that begin to grow / much larger than a fist or so." And what about organizations? Do they become enervated when they expand past a certain point? In particular, do colleges and universities function poorly as learning communities when they become very large? We believe the answer is often yes.

The growth of colleges and universities in the 1960s certainly indicated that higher education was operating in accord with the principle that bigger is better. From 1958 to 1974, total enrollment increased 300 percent; yet during the same period the number of higher education institutions increased by only 50 percent. In 1950, 75 percent of students were enrolled in colleges and universities with fewer than two thousand students; by 1974, only 30 percent were enrolled in such colleges. The massive universities emerged during this period. In 1950, only 10 institutions enrolled more than twenty thousand; by 1974, there were 95 such institutions, and their combined student bodies accounted for 30 percent of all enrollment in higher education. At the university level, 63 universities with more than twenty thousand students accounted for 70 percent of the total university enrollment.

Two other developments that frequently accompany large-scale growth were also present—concentration and centralization. The multiunit university and college, with its layers of authority, became a common phenomenon. (The language used to justify the increasing centralization of higher education was borrowed from big business advocates; college and university administrators did not discuss profits, of course, but they did argue for centralization on the grounds of increased efficiency in the use of capital and plant.) In 1950, only 15 percent of the total enrollment was in multiunit campuses, but by 1970 this figure had risen to 40 percent. These multiunit organizations emerged through voluntary merger, governmental fiat covering existing institutions, the development of new units, or by combinations of these methods. Some, such as the State University of New York (SUNY), were conglomerates with two-year as well as four-year colleges and universities. Other multiunit groups include the California systems of institutions at the same

2

level and the North Carolina conglomerate, encompassing the entire state public higher education system.

The 1970s saw the increased development of new vehicles for centralization. Statewide education boards, better known as "1202" commissions, were authorized by the federal Education Amendments of 1972. With federal encouragement, these commissions were given planning and coordinating responsibilities for all public and private postsecondary education in their respective states. Public forces shifted from higher education to postsecondary education, and with that shift the policy arena expanded to encompass area vocational schools, private trade and technical schools, museums, libraries, and a whole range of institutions—in addition to colleges and universities—that provide educational services to adults. Thus, concentration and centralization of activity and authority increased both within the enterprise and through government interaction with the enterprise.

American higher education fully demonstrated its fascination with bigness and showed little early concern for the possible negative consequences of such an interest. Many educators embraced bigger scale as a necessary prelude to increasing the benefits of college and university learning. If "economies of scale" was the watchword for maximizing return in big business, then it seemed logical that the higher education industry should be governed by the same principle of efficiency. In summarizing the economies-of-scale argument, Alexander Astin (1977, p. 245) concludes that advocates of bigger institutions "assume that facilities such as libraries and gymnasiums can be more efficiently used with large student bodies." But Astin argues that the monetary savings are "mainly illusory. Large institutions actually spend somewhat more per student for educational purposes than small institutions."

The premise that benefits result from large-scale industrial operations has not been open to serious challenge since the early stages of the industrial revolution. Certainly evidence of the benefits abounded. Mass production brought a whole range of products within reach of the entire populations of developed nations. Thus it hardly seemed necessary to question the move to large-scale enter-

3

prise in higher education when it became prevalent in the 1950s and 1960s. Many people viewed this move as a necessary concomitant of the revolution in access to higher education, which this nation set as a goal in the mid twentieth century. Mass production was seen as the only route to bring higher education to everyone. The decision to open the doors to higher education inescapably meant that more students would be behind each door. Those who accept these premises have tended to dismiss, without further examination, any attempt to question whether the benefits of large-scale educational operation were indeed real, since they consider such questioning an attack on the effort to achieve broader access to higher education.

John Gardner (in "How Big . . . ," 1970, p. vi) forcefully states the case for this view: "I have been surprised by the censorious tone with which some critics now refer to large institutions, almost as though in growing to their present size these institutions had deliberately chosen to do an evil thing. This is ridiculous. The critics may, if they wish, attack the American people for being so numerous and fertile. They may, if they wish, attack the society generally for holding such a liberal view concerning who should go to college. But they should not attack institutions that are simply trying to accomplish a well-nigh impossible task the society has handed them. The institutions being scolded for largeness today are the ones that have been most responsible to the American eagerness to broaden educational opportunities. We should have the grace to live with the consequences of our choices."

Supporters of this view seem to overlook the alternative path that could have been taken—opening more doors. To some extent that path was taken but primarily at the entry level. Of the 776 public institutions established between 1958 and 1974, more than three quarters were two-year colleges. And even though hundreds of new community colleges were opened, many existing two-year urban colleges chose to expand rather than to urge the creation of additional units. In 1974, 40 percent of all two-year-college students were enrolled in 8 percent of the two-year colleges; 81 of these institutions had enrollments in excess of ten thousand.

4

Myths of Bigger Is Better

True, the decision to greatly expand existing institutions seemed more a matter of casual acceptance than a hotly and openly debated issue. Planning documents of the period did urge better geographical distribution of institutions, and enrollment ceilings were suggested, but these ceilings were frequently revised upward as the years went on. In particular, most public universities made a conscious choice to expand rather than to limit growth, at least up to the range of twenty-five to thirty thousand students. Even when new campuses were begun, they were often within the same system and under the same governing board, but at different locations.

Comprehensiveness

Part of this willingness to accept the bigger-is-better principle was acceptance of the small-is-inferior principle. James D. Conant (1959, p. 77) gave stature to this concept as it applied to education. After studying in depth twenty-two high schools, only three of which had graduating classes of less than 100, he unequivocally concluded that "the presence of . . . high schools . . . with graduating classes of less than 100 students constitutes one of the serious obstacles to good secondary education throughout most of the United States. . . . I believe such schools are not in a position to provide a satisfactory education for any group of their students . . . the instructional program is neither sufficiently broad nor sufficiently challenging." That Conant had come to this conclusion on the basis of abstract reasoning rather than hard evidence is all too clear from his use of the phrase "the truth of this statement is self-evident." He certainly did not rely on his own findings; instead, he admonished the reader to make no generalizations from his study of the twenty-two schools because it was not random and was of insufficient size. Conant advocated *comprehensiveness,* the offering of a wide range of academic, technical, and vocational courses and programs within one institution, thereby satisfying the needs of all learners in one setting.

At the time of the Conant study, only four thousand of our twenty-one thousand high schools met his size criterion. Now that

5

we have greatly reduced the number of high schools, we are not so certain that the hoped-for benefits are being realized. A recent study by Sher and Tompkins (1976) suggests that bigger schools do not result in higher achieving students, nor do they produce students who do better in college. It is ironic that only sixteen years after Conant's report, a new report prepared for the Department of Health, Education, and Welfare, *Youth Policy in Transition,* stated that American high schools are too large.

The underlying logic for Conant's position—the need for comprehensiveness—was largely accepted by higher education. Comprehensiveness soon became a goal of community colleges, and teacher-training schools diversified and became comprehensive state colleges. Pointing out that over 30 percent of the two-year colleges in 1968 enrolled fewer than five hundred students, Medsker (1971, p. 21) says it is "not clear how such enrollment can support a viable comprehensive college operation." That the small enrollment might support some type of viable college other than a comprehensive college was not even considered worth discussing. Comprehensiveness became the standard mode for the community college.

Universities, more comprehensive than other institutions by their nature, moved still further in that direction. New professional schools were added to the traditional professions of law, medicine, and religion, departments split and spawned new departments, and research specialties and institutes multiplied. This expansion went far beyond diversification of the curriculum. Clark Kerr describes the ultimate in comprehensiveness in *The Uses of the University* (1963, pp. 7–8):

> The University of California last year had operating expenditures from all sources of nearly half a billion dollars, with almost another 100 million for construction; a total employment of over 40,000 people, more than IBM and in a far greater variety of endeavors; operations in over a hundred locations, counting campuses, experiment stations, agricultural and urban extension centers, and projects abroad involving more than fifty countries; nearly 10,000 courses in its cata-

6

logues; some form of contact with nearly every industry, nearly every level of government, nearly every person in its region. Vast amounts of expensive equipment were serviced and maintained. Over 4,000 babies were born in its hospitals. It is the world's largest purveyor of white mice. It will soon have 100,000 students—30,000 of them at the graduate level; yet much less than one third of its expenditures are directly related to teaching. It already has nearly 200,000 students in extension courses —including one out of every three lawyers and one out of every six doctors in the state.

Only the private liberal arts colleges were holdouts. Their sense of their educational mission appeared to require small scale. In the late 1950s and early 1960s, student demand was increasing more rapidly than were student places. Some small colleges did choose this period to grow substantially, but others set clear limits on growth and implicitly rejected the notion that comprehensiveness was required for their educational purpose. More explicitly, as their own internal debates testify, they were unwilling to give up certain modes of instruction—such as small classes with active student participation—and a sense of community that they believed could not be maintained on a larger scale.

The interaction of the search for comprehensiveness and large scale may be likened to a dog chasing its own tail. Since comprehensiveness is perceived as a positive goal, it is necessary to grow to sufficient size to make comprehensiveness possible, but growth tends to bring with it more diversity of interest within the larger student body. This in turn creates pressure for even greater comprehensiveness. And as the institution grows, it changes its relationship to the physical and political community of which it is a part. The use of more space, the removal of revenue-producing land from tax rolls, the visibility of students—and sometimes social problems created or exacerbated by masses of students, such as drug abuse and overcrowding of rental units—all impress on the community the need for some services to the community from the institution. If the university or college obtains support from public funds, rapid

7

growth usually results in the institutional budget's suddenly becoming a more noticeable part of the total budget allocations of the county or state. Again, this increased visibility may lead to demands for new services from the institution, either to serve more learners in the paying jurisdiction or to provide various forms of technical and research aid.

The comprehensive community college was justified, in part, by the importance of providing multiple options within one institution for students making career decisions. A student could enroll in a vocational program in medical technology, and if that did not later fit her interests and talents, she could shift to some other vocational program or to the general education program. She would not have to sever her relationship with an educational institution and apply for admission to another, with all the delay, expense, and frustration of such transactions. In effect, the student could try on, or shop for, a career and an educational program within one market. However, evidence for this type of shopping among careers in two-year colleges is relatively meager. Only 25 to 35 percent of community college enrollment is in the vocational or occupational programs. And because attrition in the first year is so high, it appears that leaving a first program choice often occurs simultaneously with leaving the institution.

Nor do students in four-year programs appear to be fully realizing the hoped-for benefits of comprehensiveness. Both Blackburn and others (1976) and Warren (1977) found that students given increased control over electives chose to specialize rather than diversify. In a large institution, the student may, in fact, have relatively little contact with programs or learners in other units. Each unit tends to function in a fairly isolated way. The excellent physics department is rarely visited by a student from the English department. Requirements for political science majors are not jointly planned with those for history majors. The potential of a rich array of subjects afforded by large scale and their contributions to the students' general undergraduate education may therefore be more illusory than real.

Comprehensiveness was not the only rationale for increasing

8

Myths of Bigger Is Better

size in higher education institutions. The concept of *critical mass*—in education, defined as the minimum concentration of scholars within a field necessary to provide adequate instruction and to generate further scholarship—was also applied, particularly to graduate schools. Certain critical masses were considered essential if quality was to be achieved. In 1969, the National Science Board set the standard of seven faculty members as the critical mass required for an adequate departmental size, although the board also cautioned that achievement of this size does not automatically lead to quality. On the basis of the board's analysis of Cartter's departmental ratings, it concluded that higher-quality departments tended to be large. (Alan Cartter [1966] devised a rating scale for graduate departments based on rankings given by peers in the field.)

A slightly different approach was employed by another researcher for linking quality to the university as a whole. Sutherland (1973), using the department as his building block, decided that a university should have twenty-five departments with an average of twenty-five faculty members in each department. By assuming that a faculty ratio of from one-to-eight to one-to-ten resulted in total enrollment of 5,000 to 6,250 for good-quality graduate education and by adding professional schools and a few other adjustments, Sutherland established the magic figure of 12,000 for a total optimum enrollment. A much lower figure could be obtained by using the National Science Board's departmental minimum together with Sutherland's number of departments; the minimum university would then be about 1,800 students, without professional schools.

The Carnegie Commission on Higher Education (1972) recommended a minimum of 5,000 students for doctoral-granting institutions. No distinction was made between graduate and undergraduate enrollment. Since few doctoral-granting institutions are exclusively graduate, it is assumed that an exclusively graduate institution could be of high quality even with an enrollment of fewer than 5,000 students. This might well explain why Rockefeller University, in New York City, although very small (about 100 students), enjoys an enviable reputation. It is possible that a university offering a narrow range of graduate programs and specializing as profes-

9

sional schools do could maintain a high-quality, though small, program.

Nonetheless, most recommendations concerning the optimum size for universities are usually based on the assumption that there need to be several graduate programs. But there is little hard evidence that, to provide a high-caliber graduate education, a university must have twenty doctoral-degree programs rather than three or four carefully selected and perhaps related programs. There may be little discernible relation between size and quality in graduate work even at the departmental level. Gallant and Prothero (1972)' examined the relation of departmental size and quality as determined by the Roose and Anderson (1970)' ratings of the quality of graduate faculties in five fields. In three fields, there was no significant relationship between size and quality. In one field, biochemistry, there was a negative relationship and in one, economics, a positive relationship (1972). Thus what appears so patently sound as a theory—the critical mass concept—finds little reinforcement in empirical data. When we can find instances of high quality without the supposed critical mass, the argument that a certain critical mass is a prerequisite for quality loses force.

Economies of Scale

The most generally accepted benefit from moving to large scale is economic, specifically the creation of *economies of scale,* referring to the reduction of the cost of producing each unit as the number of units produced is increased. Such economies are achieved because certain costs—for example, such fixed costs as buildings and equipment—do not vary over a wide range of levels of production. Applying this industrial concept to education seems reasonable, but it fails to take into account differences between producing goods and supplying services. Nonetheless, some researchers feel they have evidence of its applicability to higher education. After analyzing average costs per student at American colleges and universities, the Carnegie Commission on Higher Education (1972) concluded that with fewer than one thousand students, liberal arts colleges

10

cannot provide good liberal arts education without a limited curriculum and high unit costs. A limited curriculum is assumed to be of lower quality than a broad curriculum. But the question of how limited a curriculum can be, or how broad it should be, cannot be answered in the absence of knowledge about the student body, the mission of the institution, and the methods of pedagogy. Four-year liberal arts colleges are not sufficiently alike in these dimensions to generalize about appropriate scale in terms of either costs or quality. Furthermore, it is often too easy to equate quantity with variety. Less actual breadth may be found in an educational program consisting of ten thousand courses (the number included in the 1968 catalogue for the University of California at Berkeley), than there is in a carefully designed, integrated set of one hundred courses. After all, the ten thousand courses are spread across 27,500 students. Because of the luxury of so many students and thus the possibility of so many courses, many of the courses may be—and examination of the catalogue will indicate that they are—extremely narrow in their subject matter. The highly specialized nature of many such courses may not so much contribute to a liberal arts education as provide an early introduction to in-depth study of a discipline at the graduate level.

The Carnegie Commission pointed out that economies of scale can be found largely in administrative costs; institutional costs tend to be less sensitive to scale. Because 70 percent of the operating costs are instructional, the margin for saving in operating costs by increasing scale is relatively minor, except for very low levels of enrollment.

Capital costs are, of course, quite sensitive to scale, and very often what is identified as excessively high unit costs can be explained by overinvestment in capital at some stage in the institution's growth. This explanation is also true of the spread of fixed costs over the student body. If at some stage in the institution's growth more fixed costs were built in than were needed by the number of students and the purpose of the institution, what may masquerade as inappropriate scale is only too large a component of fixed costs. Thus faulty planning is the reason for high costs rather

11

than any inherent attribute of small scale. The growth of some experimental higher education activities in which neither substantial capital outlays (Empire State College) nor tenured faculty members (Vermont Community College) are factors demonstrates that the question of optimum scale relates far more to purpose and planning than to any immutable rules of economies of scale. Some colleges have exacerbated this problem by accepting no-layoff provisions in their collective bargaining contracts with campus labor unions. In effect, such provisions turn a variable cost into a fixed cost.

Further evidence that size does not dictate unit costs is found in the great range and generally wide dispersion of average costs shown in the scatter diagrams of average costs related to size presented by the Carnegie Commission (1971). We may too eagerly search for rules, trends, and order where in fact none prevails, at least on the basis of the variables we have singled out. Joseph A. Kershaw (1976), in *The Very Small College,* suggests an alternative hypothesis, pointing out that the Carnegie Commission's figures include a range from $750 to $3,400 for liberal arts colleges with enrollments below 500. Kershaw says, "A nonprofit institution will spend whatever money it has (plus a little more, many would say). Its efforts are devoted traditionally to increasing its income and its costs accordingly, because educational leaders are persuaded that the more they spend, the better the quality of the product. . . . Harvard has high costs not because it is large and not because it is small, but because it is rich" (1976, pp. 6–7).

Kershaw carefully studied the cost structure of three small, private liberal arts colleges with enrollments of over 500 students. And while he observed real financial problems, he concludes that "nothing inherent in the smallness of an institution accounts for financial troubles" (1976, p. 22). He points out that many of their financial problems would also be experienced by large institutions that found themselves facing declining enrollments.

Chasing economies of scale in higher education may turn out to be merely chasing a mirage. If there is no established basic unit of cost required as a threshold of quality, new financial re-

sources or changes in enrollment may lead to new levels of enrollment that could be identified as peril points in the operational scale
of educational ventures. Thus, in higher education, unit costs can
be said to be very soft, supplying us with little reliable information
about whether an operation has the best possible size, is as efficient
as it could be, or has achieved a particular level of quality. This
characteristic of softness in unit costs proves to be a very real
obstruction in obtaining federal funding for any of the bail-out
institutional aid programs talked about in the early 1970s. Who
knows when an institution is actually in trouble? If a college can
supply what is judged to be adequate education at $1,500 per
student year, why does it need to be bailed out when it is already
spending $4,500 per student year? Who knows what constitutes an
economy of scale if there is no generally accepted model that ties
unit costs to purpose and to a specified level of quality?

Again, it was the quite pervasive uncertainty about appropriate unit costs that led many researchers in the 1970s to question
the wisdom of an institutional aid program that would provide
money directly to institutions on the basis of the number of students
enrolled. A number of them observed, and perhaps rightly, that
such grants would be inflationary and little else. A large part of the
grants would be used to make larger payments to the current resources rather than to buy more resources and thereby to increase
the inputs per student and improve quality.

There has been a tendency to attribute other benefits to
large scale that might more accurately be attributed to growth
toward a larger scale. It is the growth that has been sought, not
necessarily the larger scale, even though that was the result. Growth
was considered a facilitator, if not an absolute prerequisite, for
acquiring the benefits of flexibility, diversity, prestige, and the potential for experimentation sought by many institutions.

As institutions grew, presidents gained prestige by managing
larger budgets, by hiring more personnel, and, in particular, by
being able to recruit both young faculty members and additional
administrators. Public institutions found that the state legislatures
paid more attention to them; some even worried about losing influ-

ence with the legislatures if other public institutions grew larger and had an impact on more constituents. Supervising larger budgets and more personnel justified larger salaries for upper-level administrators. But as the size increased, the administration became more specialized and professionalized. Growth in administrative power, at least in its general image and as perceived externally, was frequently accompanied by declining potential for academic leadership. Search committees looked for people who were capable of managing large budgets, not necessarily those with educational expertise and vision.

Growth was seen as essential for vitality. New blood could be recruited, new programs could be established, and experiments could be tried, as the margin provided by increasing budgets became available. But, with a few notable exceptions, the reality was that growth brought more of the same. Theoretically, greater flexibility could have been the result of budget increases, but it rarely was. Growth did permit adding more faculty, but since new recruits were selected by faculty members already there, the new recruits—at least those that remained—were very similar to their selectors. Women were seldom included in the ranks, although the earlier coincidence of rapid growth and the civil rights movement made it easier for some male minority members to be included.

Again, then, the hoped-for benefits of large scale or growth may be more myth than reality. Massive institutions were, after all, created mainly from the imposition of largely untested, but seemingly reasonable, principles or by borrowing principles from other than educational settings. That many benefits have failed to materialize is not surprising. What is more distressing is that those who wanted growth, or large scale itself, and those who accepted the notion that small was inferior now find themselves with the consequences of their decisions—a higher education system characterized by large institutions in which diseconomies of scale are beginning to be recognized.

14

CHAPTER TWO

Hidden Diseconomies of Scale

In the decades of the 1950s and 1960s, American higher education gave the lion's share of its attention to growth and expansion. With quantity as the major impetus for planning, it was all too natural to focus myopically on cost as the key unit for analysis. People who work with cost analyses very quickly begin thinking in terms of economies of scale. Higher education cost analysts were no exception, and certainly there were some economies of scale to achieve. Rarely, however, were any significant analytical power and concern devoted to the question of what educational or administrative benefits might be lost or gained as a result of changes in scale. Few research findings on this multifaceted issue are available. But it is imperative that questions about possible diseconomies of scale be

15

The Impersonal Campus

raised and studied if we are to understand the relationship between scale and quality. Some evidence is already emerging that large size has hidden costs, that diseconomies of scale do exist and should be a part of intelligent academic planning.

The term *diseconomies of scale* refers to those increased costs or losses of quality that result from the size of an operation. It is our thesis that education is particularly vulnerable to diseconomies derived from large size and that these appear earlier in educational institutions than they do in other types of enterprises. There are various types of diseconomies of scale, and in the past in education most of our attention has been focused on those related to small scale (such as the inability to make quantity purchases, to spread administrative costs, to take advantage of specialized skills). But we have often overlooked many increased costs and losses in quality related to larger-scale operations. Several types are discussed in the following pages, where we consider the impact of scale on the capacity of a college education to stimulate human development, on instructional methods, on the organization's climate and communication, and on the ability to adapt to change. That scale is a dimension of importance, with implications both for the quality of the educational process and its outcomes and for the quality of life on the campus, is, we believe, a sufficiently powerful hypothesis to warrant concern.

Student Development

Some research has been done on the relationship between personal development and institutional size in high school settings, and these studies may well have relevance for postsecondary institutions. Barker and Gump (1964) found that as schools grow, the number of persons increases much faster than either the number of learning settings or the variety of these settings. Students in small schools were involved in more activities than those in large schools and had more satisfying experiences relating to developing competence. One need only consider the role of student government officers and the opportunities for such positions in large and small

16

schools. There can be only one student body president whether the institution enrolls forty thousand or two thousand students. And yet the quality of the experience, the contribution to the development of a sense of personal responsibility, and the opportunities for working with others may be quite as useful and valid in the smaller institution as in the larger one. Opportunities to work on student newspapers and curriculum committees and to participate in performing groups, sports, and budget review committees do not increase with the number of students. In an institution with two thousand students, the chances that the students will have some possibility of taking leadership positions might reasonably be set at 1:20. At the college with forty thousand students, the ratio explodes to about 1:400.

Providing opportunities for participation in extracurricular activities is, of course, only one aspect of a college's impact on personal development. According to Newcomb's research (1962), it may be the single most important aspect, but within the educational setting there are other possibilities of aiding students' personal growth. Not the least significant of these is the opportunity of professors to work sufficiently with individual students to have some understanding of the manner in which a student attacks and solves a problem and to observe the changes in problem-solving abilities during progress through the educational system. When students in large institutions attempt to get letters of recommendation, they may discover that none of their recommenders knows more than a narrow fragment of their work at the institution, and few can attest to the range of the students' intellectual and personal abilities. The admissions committee of a graduate school may only need academic information about a relatively limited range of subjects, but when students seek employment in industry or want to enter business or training programs, they require more general letters of reference.

Another element in students' personal growth is the clarification or development of values. In particular, the development of a sense of responsibility is often set as one aim of a liberal arts education. Bowers (1964) suggests that this goal may be facilitated by small-scale educational settings. In his work on cheating, he dis-

17

The Impersonal Campus

covered that "The proportion of schools with high levels of cheating increased with the size of the school." He concludes that students at a large institution feel relatively anonymous in relation to the student body as a whole and consequently feel less responsibility to uphold community mores: Large schools "may provide a setting that facilitates the formation of deviant subgroups in which cheating is approved or at least tolerated" (1964, p. 30). Students should reach that stage of maturity in which the exercise of responsibility is not influenced by the size of their group or the degree of anonymity they experience, but perhaps the full-fledged acquisition of responsibility can only come after development and exercise in more discrete and supportive transitional settings.

Other things being equal, small colleges produce more desirable changes in students than do large institutions (Bowen, 1977). And small size is also positively associated with college persistence.

Instruction and Evaluation

The greatest impacts of size are likely to be felt in the techniques of instruction, including the testing and assessment of students. The huge introductory lecture classes of several hundred students are an economy-of-scale temptation made possible by massive institutions. Although they are not without value, too many such courses in the formative first two years of a college student's life can strongly reinforce all tendencies toward passive learning and give little or no aid to the development of an active, participating learner. At most large institutions, the small discussion class is saved for upper-division students. But by the junior year many students have already established a pattern of simply listening and taking notes. The failure of students to develop a sense of responsibility for active participation in the learning process and the consequent reduced possibilities for internalizing learning and for refining their understanding through discussions with peers and course instructors may well be casualties of giving more attention to achieving economies of scale than to the impact of various methods of instruction on learning attitudes.

18

Hidden Diseconomies of Scale

How students judge the quality of their instruction in institutions or classes of different sizes is indicated by two studies. According to Astin and Lee (1972), students at large institutions give lower overall ratings and lower specific ratings on personal contacts with students and faculty, freedom in course selection, and the quality of instruction than do students at small colleges. And students' ratings on how much they have learned in a course and how effectively the instructor has encouraged them to become actively involved in learning are negatively related to class size. The highest ratings are given in classes of five to twenty-five students, somewhat lower ratings in classes of twenty-five to fifty students, and lower again in classes of fifty to one hundred students. Classes of one hundred or more received the lowest ratings (Crittenden, Norr, and LeBailly, 1975).

That instructional techniques associated with large institutions do indeed result in losses of quality has not been established, however. Efforts to settle this issue have been so inconclusive or have suggested such slight differences that they have discouraged more investigation. Dubin and Traveggia (1968), after reviewing ninety-one research projects completed between 1924 and 1965, concluded: "These data demonstrate clearly and unequivocally that there is no measurable difference among truly distinctive methods of college instruction when evaluated by student performance on final examination."

The aspect of instruction that is clearly affected by class size, and to some extent by institutional size, is the range of assessment techniques available to the faculty. Even the person who does the evaluation may be a function of class size. The shift toward "objective" examinations was almost necessitated by the growth in scale of many educational settings. There are college graduates today who have rarely, if ever, written a sentence in response to a question and even more who have never responded to a question with a paragraph, let alone written papers. Because of the limitations of such assessment techniques as the multiple-choice test, students lose valuable opportunities for practice in writing and the faculty loses the opportunity to aid students in developing the writing skills that

19

will be needed in the years after college. Ironically, we are now beginning to develop a whole range of evaluation methods, including the use of juries and observation panels, self-assessment, and peer assessment, at a time when many institutions and many of their courses are far too large to consider using these techniques. Educators who argue that the evaluation of a student's progress should be used as much for instructional purposes as for evaluation purposes can only be disappointed by large educational settings in which the examination or the evaluation is quite separate from instruction and serves only to test. In such a situation the potential of evaluation as a tool for learning cannot be realized.

Institutional Climate

The adverse effects of large scale may be most demonstrable in the climate of a campus, although many other factors of course contribute to the atmosphere besides size. Both class size and institutional size seem to be important components of a climate that motivates the student and enhances learning. Describing those structural attributes and faculty and student characteristics that correlated with high ratings on a criterion labeled "concern for the individual student," Bayer (1975, p. 557) notes that size was the "attribute most highly correlated with the criterion: the larger the institution, the less was the concern for the individual student." He concludes his study with a strong statement: "Clearly, having a highly credentialed, productive, and research-oriented faculty does nothing to create the impression that the institution is concerned with the individual student, an environmental measure which is related to student learning, to educational persistence and aspirations, and to student discontent or satisfaction. . . . If the institution's structure—particularly its size—persists as a strong determinant of the institutional environment . . . these results support Gallant and Prothero's thesis that institutional growth beyond some optimal limits leads to alienation, absence of community, and numerous other outcomes which are dysfunctional for all members of the campus community and are not subject to the control of the administrators or the efforts of the faculty" (1975, p. 562).

Student protest may also be seen as an expression of an institution's climate. And we do know that student protest occurs more often and has a greater effect at larger colleges than at smaller ones. In a major study of the campus outbreaks over the U.S. military intervention in Cambodia (Peterson and Bilorusky, 1971), colleges were divided into four groups according to size: less than 1,000, 1,000–5,000, 5,000–12,000, and more than 12,000 students. Measures of the perceived significant impact of the outbreaks on campus operations yielded a 41.3 percent for the group of smallest institutions, rising to 89.9 percent for the group of largest institutions. An even wider range of difference was revealed by analyzing the incidence of extreme actions, including strikes and destructive demonstrations. This study also revealed, however, that student protests can have important positive results and that both the likelihood of positive effects and their extent appear to be related to size. The percentage of college presidents who belived protest benefited teaching and learning on their campuses was almost twice as high at small colleges as it was at very large institutions. The presidents of small colleges were also more impressed that students had acquired an increased concern about national and international problems than were their counterparts at larger institutions.

The personal/impersonal dimension of an institution's climate may even be a factor in the number of lawsuits that students and faculty members bring against colleges and universities. Increasingly, complaints about discrimination, the rights of students as consumers, and due process are taken to court. Although we have seen no systematic study of how the size of an institution is related to the number of complaints filed that could not be settled at the institutional level without going to court, an examination of a listing of such cases does suggest that complaints at the larger institutions are more likely to reach the courts. Larger institutions may feel that they can withstand the expense and risks of a prolonged lawsuit, but it could also be that the departmentalization and impersonality of a large institution make it harder to reach satisfactory out-of-court agreements.

Communication

Whether students have many opportunities to discuss with each other their educational experiences may affect their ultimate learning, and here again, size seems to be an influential variable. McKeachie and Borden (1961) point out that "in a large college the statistical chances that another student in the same class will be in the same living group are smaller than in a small college. Students in a large college with many courses, and even many sections of the same course, have few common intellectual experiences. Consequently, it is difficult for them to communicate about intellectual problems outside of class." Small residential colleges that have retained small classes and a somewhat structured general curriculum undoubtedly afford students the greatest number of chances to form relatively stable subgroups in which shared educational experiences can be discussed. Of course, as the small college imitates its larger counterparts by moving toward large classes and eliminates many features of dormitory life, such as changing to central dining, the educational advantages may disappear. Conversely, if the larger college makes efforts to create appropriate opportunities and has a curriculum in which at least a part of the educational experience is shared by substantial numbers of students, the disadvantages of its size may also disappear.

In any organization, effective communication is an essential element of institutional development. Unless all members of an organization understand the purposes of management actions or new programs, students and faculty members alike tend at best to be confused and at worst paranoid about the possible negative effects of these actions on them or their programs. And managers must also have ways of knowing how the faculty, students, and alumni are responding to problems and proposed actions. When an institution is too large for frequent all-college meetings, and for many face-to-face communications at all levels, the administrative memo takes

22

over. In an academic setting the administrative memo is grossly inadequate. Numerous misinterpretations can gain currency, and myriad clarifications and amplifications must then be issued.

If there are too many layers between top policy makers and those who must implement policy, the layers may serve to distort both the policy and the generally accepted image of its makers. In this situation, units tend to become isolated from each other, and there may be a divorce of administrative segments from the central purposes of the institution. The units may be inclined to create their own aims, sometimes without relevance to the central goal of the institution. Thus an accounting office may create a sophisticated and expensive operation for its own unit but one that fails to provide useful information for an educational enterprise. Or an academic department might hire very theoretically oriented faculty members, while the admissions office, in the interest of doing its job by filling student places, may be recruiting students who want and expect to take highly practical courses. Where the organizational structure of a unit has become fragmented, it is entirely possible for each unit to serve its own ends rather than those of the institution as a whole.

Adaptability

Colleges and universities, like any other organism, must find a way to maintain their stability and their vitality. Vitality requires some capacity for change and adaptation as the institution's own environment makes different demands and produces different ingredients for the life of the institution. In our work at the Fund for the Improvement of Postsecondary Education, we were soon impressed with the fact that the small institutions seemed more capable of creating that nucleus of energy essential for any change. They were more frequently able to identify their purposes so that change could take place within the framework of those aims. An institution can maintain integrity of purpose while changing some of its processes and activities to better accomplish its goals. Stability can be achieved by organizations in a variety of ways. There is no doubt that bureaucratization and insularity of subunits within an organization aid in maintaining the status quo. The stability thus achieved is, however, much more a stability of process rather than of purpose. It may be that the genius of adaptability that can be shown within a framework of broader stability cannot exist in large-scale organizations. Ladd (1972, pp. 215–216) relates size to the capacity for bringing about change in educational policies:

> Realization of these possible improvements probably depends upon one or both of two conditions: leadership and appropriate size. . . . Readiness for change rarely, if ever, simply emerges—especially in large, complex organizations. Someone must work to develop it. . . . Someone must provide for political management and insure that it is functioning effectively. . . . In the context of the collegial system, it does seem reasonable to assert that leadership is more likely to emerge and to be effective if the decision-making unit is not too large nor too heterogeneous. Awareness of the need of change and ability to deal with principles and to have a manageable political process are all more likely in a group that is small enough to permit regular interaction among members and which is sufficiently homogeneous to rest upon shared goals and objectives. These are, after all, the essence of the collegial system. I do not suggest that small size in homogeneity alone will insure that the process of change will be successful. My studies indicate that the critical points in the process are just as critical in small situations as in the multiversity and require just as much that someone take charge. But the likelihood that someone will do so seems to be much less in one of our large heterogeneous institutions. We should, I think, be giving our best efforts to finding ways of reducing the size and extreme diversity of our decision-making units primarily as a means toward permitting the development and functioning of effective leadership.

The points raised in this chapter undoubtedly constitute only the tip of the iceberg of possible diseconomies of large-scale educational institutions. Clearly, more information is needed on these phenomena. We are not launching a movement to dismantle our large institutions, because their scale does seem to provide some educational and economic benefits that may be difficult to acquire in small settings. But we are stating emphatically that further investigation of diseconomies of scale will aid us in better understanding the best use and management of both large- and small-scale institutions.

CHAPTER THREE

Increasing
Learning Options
Without Expansion

One historical argument for the expansion of colleges and universities into larger and larger institutions has been the presumed educational benefits that are accommodated within a large enterprise. Big institutions provide students with a greater range of courses, curriculums, faculty models, and peers than can be found in smaller settings. Recently, Blackburn and others (1976) have questioned whether students actually take advantage of this plethora of opportunities. But it is nonetheless true that diversity has been traditionally associated with large size. Under a larger umbrella there is simply room for more. However, is it also axiomatic that only giant-sized institutions can provide students with a variety of educational programs?

Over the past decade, small colleges have discovered that they can offer students more options without significantly changing their size, structure, or basic purposes. Through a variety of voluntary arrangements, informal agreements, and negotiated alliances (some more entangling than others), these schools have expanded their teaching faculties, course offerings, library holdings, laboratory facilities, and even their physical plant while retaining the basic characteristics of small scale. This chapter describes several recent efforts to maximize educational options for students within smaller colleges to demonstrate what is being done to achieve the benefits of large-scale institutions without some of their attendant liabilities.

During the past fifty years, colleges have entered into formal cooperative arrangements for a variety of reasons, usually related to reducing costs and making maximum use of existing facilities. The first nationally acknowledged interinstitutional consortium of small colleges, the Claremont Center, began in 1925, when the president of Pomona College suggested that several schools share a common library to minimize needless duplication of resources (F. Patterson, 1973). In 1929, the Atlanta University Center was founded to ease the transition from undergraduate to graduate education for students in predominantly black institutions in Georgia. It also served to enrich the faculty's educational opportunities by encouraging cooperative research activities and exchanges among Clark, Morris Brown, Spelman, and Morehouse Colleges and Atlanta University.

Between 1930 and the 1960s, the formal *consortia movement* among colleges, as Lewis Patterson has termed it, grew steadily, if not remarkably. By 1967, there were thirty-one operating consortia, which each met Patterson's five criteria (1975):

1. A voluntary formal organization
2. Three or more member institutions
3. Multi-academic programs
4. Administration by at least one full-time professional

5. An annual contribution or other tangible evidence of long-term commitment from member institutions

The big explosion in the number of formal consortia occurred in the 1970s. Between 1970 and 1977, nearly half of the more than 120 formally recognized existing consortia were established, and another dozen were forming (Patterson, 1977, p. 11). One explanation for the development of these interinstitutional arrangements is that administrators believed that through collaboration institutions could save money. Small wonder then that the movement caught on at a time when colleges, especially the smaller institutions, faced declining budgets, decreasing enrollments, and rising costs. The Carnegie Commission on Higher Education (1972, p. 127) echoed the administrators' hopes when it asserted, "Significant economies can be achieved through consortium arrangements and other forms of interinstitutional cooperation."

The only problem with this argument on behalf of building consortia is that the hoped-for economic benefits have not yet materialized (Quehl, 1972). As the College Center of the Finger Lakes, a consortium of four institutions in New York State, has concluded, "There is little evidence that interinstitutional cooperation has led to great savings or economies" (Breneman, 1976, p. 53). The growing concern over finding ways to measure the cost-effectiveness of consortia led the Carnegie Foundation to award a two-year project grant to the Council for Interinstitutional Leadership in 1977 to undertake a study of the economies of consortia. The project's purpose is to identify and validate exemplary cooperation programs that provide cost savings and cost effectiveness; data for the study will be gathered about a variety of institutional functions, including joint purchasing, cross-registration, library cooperation, academic planning, continuing education, and off-campus programs. Researchers are only now beginning to develop formulas for revealing the economic differences in doing things cooperatively as opposed to unilaterally.

While the debate over the economic advantages of consortia rages on, critics also wonder whether even modest benefits to insti-

29

tutions outweigh the loss in institutional autonomy. They lament the creation of yet another layer of red tape and bureaucracy that stands between decisions and their implementation. Advocates of consortia, however, urge schools to compute the cost of the enhanced product if offered by the single institution in order to establish reductions in unit cost. Such efforts may legitimately be criticized as artificial; actual consortia costs are compared with single-campus costs that probably would never have been incurred. Thus, the purported savings are often illusory at best.

However, exclusive attention to costs obscures what may be the most important value of consortia: interinstitutional arrangements have provided educational benefits to students, particularly undergraduates, which could not otherwise have been available at small colleges. As two researchers have recently written, "Multicampus programs, regionally organized or otherwise, do not necessarily save money, but they do hold the promise of giving students and faculty program options not otherwise available" (Bowen and Lee, 1971, p. 13).

Looking over the entire range of types of agreements, collaborations, and consortia, one detects a number of educational purposes to which cooperative activity may be directed. The three most common objectives are: (1) to increase an institution's ability to respond to students' *specialized,* often newly emerging, interests; (2) to increase an institution's academic *comprehensiveness;* and (3) to enhance student learning options through the effective use of noncollegiate resources. At first glance, the first two purposes may seem identical in the sense that each eventually means that a small college can offer more to its undergraduates. There is, however, an important difference in emphasis. For example, the establishment of a collaborative women's studies program, such as the one currently being designed and implemented by the Great Lakes Colleges Association, uses cooperation to mount a special program that none of the twelve institutions would or probably could, economically, do by themselves. This model creates something that did not exist at any of the member colleges previously. While the women's studies program results in some greater comprehensiveness, the impetus is the newly identified specialized interest.

Collaborations designed to increase the comprehensiveness of institutions usually are less sharply focused on programs; instead they use mechanisms for cross-registration, joint degree programs, shared library and laboratory facilities, and access to a variety of extracurricular activities. This model to expand comprehensiveness more closely approximates the presumed advantages of a large university than does the collaboration that focuses on developing a new, specialized educational program. Collaborations that have comprehensiveness as their goal are strengthened when the participating schools represent differing academic strengths and vocational emphasis.

One of the most interesting of this type of collaboration links a vocational community college in upstate New York—Broome Community College—with the liberal arts college of the State University of New York at Binghamton. Fortunately, the two institutions are in close proximity, and so students may attend classes at either school with relative ease. No new programs have been established, but the range of course offerings commonly afforded liberal arts majors in their senior year has been greatly expanded. Similarly, students at Broome are able to take a greater variety of traditional introductory liberal arts courses than is offered at the community college. We will discuss these different models in greater detail later on.

While the number of formal consortia grew in the past few years, other forms of voluntary cooperation between two or more small colleges have been in existence for decades. These cooperative arrangements do not meet Patterson's criteria for consortia. Like the collaborations for new specialized interests, these cooperative arrangements are also frequently program specific but differ in that the focus is on off-campus activities. Such arrangements constitute a third purpose for forming collaborations. For example, joint internship and junior year abroad programs made it possible for students enrolled in small colleges to participate in off-campus

31

learning activities that did not place a heavy financial burden on any single institution. One typical arrangement between institutions might include the sharing of administrative costs to place student interns from a number of colleges with members of Congress. A single staff member interviews prospective job candidates and employers and arranges mutually beneficial work experiences. This model was developed by Wellesley and Vassar colleges in 1955 for their Washington summer internship program. Both schools felt it was in their best interests to cooperate. Furthermore, the arrangement reduced some of the anxiety for students who were competing for a limited number of placements; one person with good contacts was working for everyone. In addition, colleges geographically isolated from urban centers like Washington find it advantageous to work through local institutions to provide housing, guidance, and even classroom-based seminars while their students participate in these internship programs. Thus, small colleges enter into cooperative agreements with larger schools, such as American University in Washington or New York University, to provide an education to students away from the home campus.

The most widely used mechanism of interinstitutional collaboration that does not conform to Patterson's criteria for consortia is the joint junior year abroad programs sponsored by more than five hundred small colleges and universities throughout the country. Most small schools do not have their own facilities abroad, and thus they rely on the resources of other colleges. Frequently colleges focus on foreign study in one locale, such as the Irish studies in Dublin sponsored by Manhattan College. Manhattan students wishing to go abroad elsewhere use already existing programs at a sister institution. Examples of this kind of flexible but carefully planned use of extra-campus resources include the Hamilton College program in France, the Antioch College centers in Mexico and Italy, the Stanford program in England, and the recently negotiated Hebrew University/ State University of New York contract for student exchange both within the collaborating university systems and for students from other colleges and universities. Recent estimates suggest that fifty colleges and universities have taken advantage of the Stanford and

Increasing Learning Options Without Expansion

Hamilton programs alone. Obviously, this type of interinstitutional arrangement exists for very limited purposes, and no single small institution can hope to create the diversity of courses or educational opportunities offered by larger schools simply by developing a network of junior year abroad contacts. However, in many respects, the junior year abroad program serves as an important but often overlooked model of interinstitutional collaboration for less global activities. Now let us reexamine these forms of collaboration more closely.

Specialized Consortia

In this brief examination of the kinds of voluntary associations in which small colleges engage, it is disturbing to note that so few are developed to focus on a special need. Perhaps the mere suggestion of collaboration inevitably leads administrators to think in bigger terms rather than in smaller, more particularized, units. Yet much can be done to improve a college simply by adding new fields of specialization not currently offered in the curriculum. One common misconception about specialized consortia is that the institutions must be close together for students to take advantage of the program. This is often advantageous but not necessary in all cases. The Five Colleges, Inc., in Massachusetts is a widely recognized model of a collaboration to enhance individual institutions' ability to offer specialized fields.

Although this collaboration of four small private colleges— Smith, Amherst, Hampshire, and Mt. Holyoke—and one public university, the University of Massachusetts, also facilitates cross-registration for students at all campuses, it has recently focused on the establishment of joint faculty appointments among the five institutions to promote teaching and scholarship in particular fields. The fact that no school is more than fifteen miles from the farthest neighbor makes it possible for students to take courses at more than one campus. Nevertheless, this Five Colleges model can and is being adapted to settings where schools do not enjoy geographical proximity, such as the Great Lakes Colleges Association.

The program of joint faculty appointment allows the mem-

33

ber institutions to create an academic concentration through cooperation in a manner they would not be able to offer on their own. Comparable departments or interdisciplinary councils representing all five institutions establish academic priorities—those areas they believe need strengthening on their individual campuses. In most cases, this has meant adding one faculty member to integrate disparate courses taught on a number of campuses. In a few cases, the setting of priorities has meant putting together an entirely new set of courses and academic experiences to develop a program from scratch. Faculty members are appointed for two- or three-year periods; all resulting courses and activities are open to students from all five institutions. One institution serves as the host for each appointee, but staff members of the joint faculty appointment program teach courses on all five campuses. Any institution may, when a person completes the initial appointment, establish a permanent position on its own if it so desires. To date, three persons from the program have been hired in tenured appointments. In 1977, the Five Colleges, Inc., awarded tenure for the first time to one of the faculty members from the program; this individual now holds a professorship in the Five Colleges organization. In all, twelve joint appointments have been made during the past three years in such specialized and interdisciplinary fields as Latin American art and archaeology, South Asian studies, technology studies, women's studies, and medical ethics.

It is not difficult to ascertain the benefits of this strategy to the institutions involved. The schools each pay only one fifth of the cost of a faculty member to teach full time. The model also serves as a low-risk mechanism for testing the feasibility of a new concentration before the colleges must make difficult, long-term commitments of faculty positions and funds. Indirectly, the joint appointments program has enhanced faculty development at each institution. Since most of the colleges sport dangerously high tenure ratios for their faculty, the addition of someone familiar with the scholarship in a newly burgeoning field of study, such as women's history, helps older faculty members reassess their own syllabuses and teaching techniques.

34

Increasing Learning Options Without Expansion

Perhaps the most convincing test of the value of the joint appointments program lies with the students, who see it as a mechanism for enhancing their education. Since initial support for the project came from the Fund for the Improvement of Postsecondary Education, the program had to evaluate its impact. The evaluation report, submitted in 1976, reveals that both currently enrolled students at member institutions of the Five Colleges, Inc., and students considering attending one of these colleges view the collaboration as a "major factor" in their choice of college. Prospective applicants noted that they intended to take advantage of the entire Five Colleges program (including cross-registration) if they came, and a majority of undergraduates noted that they considered the collaboration one of the factors that kept them enrolled in one of the five schools (Burn, 1976). Of course, undergraduates did not take advantage of the program equally, and the students that did were not evenly distributed among the schools. Fewer students from the private colleges attended the University of Massachusettts than the reverse. Also, the joint appointments program appealed to a smaller group of students than did the general provisions for cross-registration and shared library facilities. But those students who commented on the availability of the specialized programs were among the most enthusiastic in their praise for the Five Colleges model. Five Colleges, Inc., which incorporates the development of specialized curriculums, is but one approach to the use of collaborations and consortia for specialization.

Another approach to offering a particular field of study that differs in organization and emphasis from the Five Colleges construct has been implemented by Spertus College of Judaica, in Chicago, with a number of colleges and universities throughout the Midwest. Spertus has taken the lead in offering Judaic studies to students enrolled at institutions that do not offer it themselves. Students at nearby institutions, such as Mundelein, Loyola, Northwestern, and the University of Chicago, are able to enroll at Spertus for courses that would not ordinarily be available unless they were full-time theological or rabbinical students at Spertus. Students who come from outside the Chicago area enroll for a semester or even

35

a year at Spertus to complete a concentration in Judaic studies. Frequently these students are enrolled in theology and religion programs at small sectarian institutions, which do not have the resources or staff to offer a concentration in non-Christian religion. Unlike the Five Colleges model, the Spertus arrangement exists solely to provide a special education program to students who would not enroll at Spertus themselves but need a *part* of what that institution can offer; also, the collaboration is not based on geographical proximity. Currently more than two dozen small colleges and moderate-size universities, both graduate and undergraduate, have developed formal arrangements with Spertus. Although Spertus and its collaborators have yet to work out such issues as tuitions and student fees, this arrangement is nevertheless a solution to the problem facing an increasing number of small institutions that wish to integrate a sizeable specialized curriculum with their existing offerings. One can imagine a number of variations on this theme being enacted successfully.

Keller Graduate School of Management, one of Spertus' sister institutions in Chicago, has worked out a similar kind of collaboration with members of the Associated Colleges of the Midwest (ACM) consortium. The ACM colleges, private schools offering a traditional liberal arts curriculum, have devised a program with Keller to provide management courses and training for students either in the summer between their junior and senior years or for as long as an academic year; in the latter case, the program is treated as a minor field complementing their liberal arts major. The program was designed in particular to help women students at the ACM colleges obtain a much-needed introduction to the world of business and graduate study in management. Since Keller does not have an undergraduate program, it does not threaten the basic sequence of the ACM students' academic program. It merely gives the colleges a chance to provide a specialized education for students who need to integrate their liberal arts education with the world of work. Although the program has been in operation less than two years, other small liberal arts colleges—among them, the members

Increasing Learning Options Without Expansion

of the Great Lakes Colleges Association (GLCA)—have already begun to explore ways of participating with Keller and ACM.

GLCA appears to be one of the most successful and aggressively collaborating of the small college groups in the country. It has pursued the benefits of cooperative activity in a variety of ways, including a faculty development program, urban internships, curriculum development, joint institutes, film workshops, and special teaching fellowships. Perhaps one reason for the collaboration's high record of joint achievement is the isolation of each of the campuses. Twelve institutions, spread over three states, belong to the GLCA: Albion, Antioch, Denison, DePauw, Earlham, Hope, Kalamazoo, Kenyon, Oberlin, Ohio Wesleyan, Wabash, and Wooster. The closest of the twelve, the College of Wooster and Denison, are thirty miles apart; the two farthest institutions, Kalamazoo and DePauw, are more than five hundred miles from each other. In many respects, despite their geographical distances, these colleges are remarkably similar in tradition, campus life, and academic reputation. If they were closer together, they might be in greater competition with each other for student enrollment. Eleven out of the twelve are small (fewer than twenty-five hundred students), private coeducational colleges that were founded during the late eighteenth and the nineteenth century by religious or alternative communities, such as the abolitionists who founded Oberlin. Wabash, a men's college, is the only single-sex institution of the group. (Kenyon, formerly all-male, went coeducational in 1972.) The three nationally known institutions in the consortium are Antioch, Oberlin, and Earlham colleges, but the other institutions have good regional reputations and generally do not take a deferential position to these three.

The GLCA has used the homogeneity of its students—primarily white, Protestant, and middle class—and the homogeneity of the campus life—residential, quiet, reflective, and academic—as bases from which to build a collaboration that exposes students to learning activities not frequently encountered on the home campus. Students may study art in New York City for a semester or become involved in urban renewal in Philadelphia. These programs are now, after a decade, well established and self-sufficient. One new activity for the GLCA is the development of a special joint-degree program in women's studies to be offered by the consortium itself. Presently no single institution in the association is financially capable of developing women's studies into a coherent academic program, although all the member institutions include courses about women in their curriculums.

The idea for a consortium-wide program emerged from the work of faculty members who, under a faculty development program sponsored by the Lilly Foundation, convened a GLCA Women's Studies Committee in 1975. In January 1977, 100 participants from the twelve institutions gathered at a workshop to learn how to design and teach women's studies courses. As a result of two years of planning, the faculty is mounting a major, or concentration, in women's studies. Students from any of the member campuses will be able to elect a sequence of courses, practicums, and life-planning workshops, which will form the basis of the concentration. The program is being developed with the cooperation of the career planning centers at the colleges so that faculty members will be able to advise women students about work opportunities beyond graduate and professional studies.

One unusual feature of the women's studies program is the appointment of a GLCA visiting scholar—a senior academic appointment that carries both teaching and program development responsibilities. The visiting scholar resides at one campus each semester and serves as a "circuit rider" helping each college strengthen its own educational resources for women as well as its contribution to the consortium's program. The GLCA is receiving partial support from the Fund for the Improvement of Postsecondary Education for the visiting scholar position, which is being filled in 1978–79 by Florence Howe, professor of humanities at SUNY Old Westbury and a pioneer in the development of women's studies programs nationally.

Our purpose is not to discuss the merits of women's studies as a distinct undergraduate major or concentration, but the history

38

of women in culture and society must be integrated into the existing undergraduate curriculum. Many of the GLCA institutions have less than a dozen tenured women on their faculties and have even fewer men who are consciously "writing" women into their courses or using textbooks that present an accurate picture of the roles men and women have played. GLCA women faculty members who teach such courses as "Women in Literature" and "Women in History" are often isolated from recent research in these new fields. The pioneers of these courses are already overburdened with the responsibility of teaching the entire course load of women's studies for their particular institutions.

The consortium approach to the interdisciplinary concern of women's studies makes it possible for faculty members to plan and rationalize a coherent program while acquiring a new depth and understanding of the relationship of scholarship on women to their own disciplines. A women's studies model might be applied to a variety of so-called interdisciplinary topics, such as environmental studies; urban affairs; science, technology, and ethics programs; comparative languages; and medieval studies. These areas of study are probably too specialized for individual colleges to develop on their own. Yet smaller institutions can effect some of the depth commonly associated with larger research-oriented institutions simply by working together.

Although much of the preceding discussion has the unmistakable ring of reasonableness, a mystery remains about why more of this kind of collaboration is not being tried throughout the country. Perhaps many colleges think they are collaborating merely by letting students register for courses elsewhere. The most common responses to student queries about taking a specialized major unavailable on the home campus are "Why don't you transfer for a year?" or "Why don't you develop an independent major?" Both replies suggest that it is the student who must reach out, with little effort by the institution itself. Clearly colleges cannot respond with a new program or a consortium every time a student demands a specialized curriculum, but repeated requests for a concentration in a specific field should elicit some institutional planning and effort to facilitate and augment the student's initiative.

Comprehensive Consortia

The desire of small colleges to add a variety of different courses to their individual curriculums is perhaps the most frequent impetus for building consortia. One has simply to look at the numbers of small-college collaborations which pride themselves on procedures for cross-registration, shared library and laboratory facilities, and joint extracurricular programs to recognize that when most administrators talk of the benefits of cooperation, they refer to the capacity of a consortium to provide *comprehensiveness*. Educators generally believe that the simplest way to enhance their college's comprehensiveness is to give students a chance to take a greater range of courses and programs of study. Thus, not surprisingly, cross-registration is perhaps the single most common feature of collaborations and consortia. In a recent study of the cross-registration procedures of the Pittsburgh Council on Higher Education, both students and faculty members indicated that cross-registration gives students a new academic viewpoint, a varied social experience, and a broader base of course offerings (Rush, 1977). During 1975–76 in one typical smaller consortium, the Associated Colleges of the St. Lawrence Valley, students cross-registered for a total of 323 different courses. The five participating colleges would have required thirty-eight additional faculty members to have provided their students the same options on campus as were made possible through the consortium (Grupe, 1976).

One might assume that cross-registration in larger consortia would involve even greater numbers of courses. However, as Lewis Patterson and other researchers have pointed out, the wider the geographical area and the bigger the consortium's size, the more likely it is that, beyond a certain point of convenience, cross-registration in practice does not add as many options as it appears to on paper. "Bigness tends to lead to fragmentation," Patterson (1975, p. 11) notes. Also, cross-registration tends to be inhibited

40

in large consortia because of differences in course scheduling, grading procedures, and academic calendars. The paradox is that consortia with the greatest potential for enhancing the comprehensiveness of the curriculum at each college have the greatest difficulty in establishing common cross-registration procedures.

Cross-registration runs more smoothly in settings where institutions and faculties have similar learning processes. For example, the Associated Colleges of Central Kansas includes six church-related, private liberal arts institutions, which have all adopted a common 4-1-4 calendar facilitating student mobility among campuses for programs and courses. Yet to a large extent, the schools are more alike in their curricular offerings than different; and so although cross-registration in this collaboration creates the appearance of comprehensiveness, little additional variety is actually provided.

Thus, the collaborations that work may not provide enough diversity; the ones that incorporate a diversity of institutions often do not work. In any consortium, each school has its stronger and weaker academic departments, and therefore courses appearing exactly alike in each college's catalogue may be taught quite differently. This difference in quality raises problems about determining the effectiveness of collaborations for the purpose of enhancing the comprehensive nature of the undergraduate curriculum. Schools with similar traditions, academic status, and educational goals are more likely to collaborate than dissimilar institutions but consortia that include a variety of institutional types have the most potential for maximizing learning options for students. The members of a consortium like the Associated Colleges of the Mid-Hudson Area, in southeastern New York, have little in common except their geographical location. These twenty-four institutions of higher education (five public and nineteen private; five two-year and nineteen four-year) might conceivably find ways to broaden and strengthen their capacity to offer students a comprehensive program rivaling that of many larger institutions, but they would have difficulty establishing mutually acceptable procedures.

The question then becomes how to get small clusters of postsecondary education institutions that are markedly different from one another to work to *complement*, not duplicate, each other's strengths. Indeed, comprehensiveness might be achieved more easily through the intense collaboration of two schools with seemingly incompatible, and even contradictory, educational goals than through a loose and unarticulated confederation of many different institutions or a tightly controlled arrangement between highly similar ones. The key feature of what we call *unlikely collaborations* is that two or more dissimilar institutions band together to expose students to courses and programs that would not ordinarily be a part of their education at that institution.

One such collaboration linking different types of institutions is the joint-degree program, a cooperative arrangement between Harpur College of SUNY at Binghamton and Broome Community College. Under this program, students at Harpur can work simultaneously toward both a liberal arts bachelor's degree and a vocationally oriented associate in applied science degree at Broome Community College, while Broome students can study liberal arts at a more specialized level. This program reverses the traditional sequence in which community college students transfer "up" to a four-year college. In fact, graduates from community colleges frequently do not go on to complete traditional liberal arts educations, preferring to apply their specialized training immediately to work. In the Harpur-Broome model, comprehensiveness provides a chance for junior and senior liberal arts students to concentrate in a related technical field taught at a two-year institution. For example, students in this program major in geology and civil technology or in drama and electrical technology (Stannard, 1977).

A similar program has been implemented at Henderson State University, in Arkadelphia, Arkansas, in collaboration with local vocational-technical schools. Their joint-degree program leads to an associate degree in career studies upon the completion of thirty hours of liberal arts courses and thirty hours of vocational training. Students can complete the two parts of the degree *simultaneously*, since both parts of the program are offered at each institution, or they can complete the program sequentially. Both the New York and the Arkansas joint-degree programs enhance the capacity of the participating schools to offer students a comprehensive education, one that means exposure to both a liberal education and training for a particular vocation.

These particular arrangements for comprehensiveness alter traditional patterns and assumptions about higher education. Juniors in a liberal arts college are not expected to take courses at a community college when, by all rights, they have finished the first two years of their college education. Indeed, if these programs were strictly collaborations within a traditional liberal arts framework, the arrangement would make no sense. However, the courses offered by each school are quite different; a two-year program in medical laboratory technology does not repeat the first two years of a biology major, for example.

One important benefit of these unlikely collaborations is that liberal arts faculty members found that they did not lose student enrollments in major fields. Traditional liberal arts education appeared to be strengthened by permitting students to sample both forms and then perceive the value of each. "There is evidence," one study concludes, "that the joint-degree program contributes to the preservation of liberal arts education. . . . [It] has the important outcome of qualifying its graduates for employment without compromising or interfering with their liberal arts education" (Stannard, 1977, p. 14). Perhaps a graduate summed it up best when she noted that although her work tasks involved skills learned at the community college, "the analytical skills developed in the four-year liberal arts program permitted me to evaluate these tasks."

Consortia for Off-Campus Learning

Numerous colleges join together each year to provide off-campus learning opportunities for students. One need only think of the internship programs and junior year abroad activities mentioned earlier to realize that collaborations that focus on off-campus learning have been among the most successful of all cooperative ventures (Carnegie Commission on Higher Education, 1971). The reasons are obvious. These programs do not pose a threat to departmental enrollments, since they usually occur between terms or during summer vacations. Even the junior year abroad frequently means that language departments benefit from offering students this option, which serves as a lure to increase the number of foreign language majors. Also, these collaborations add a dimension to a college's curriculum without committing the institution to joint planning of other courses; they do not tamper with a school's autonomy or freedom to operate in any way it chooses. There are few, if any, strings attached to consortia that do not alter existing campus programs but do enhance a student's noncollegiate learning experiences.

This type of collaboration frequently entails the sharing of facilities (such as a residence in a foreign country) or staff (such as internship placement officers). One school may own the off-campus site and operate it on a fee basis for a variety of participating institutions, a common arrangement in junior year abroad programs. Sometimes the consortium itself owns or operates the program independently from any single institution's control. For example, the College Center of the Finger Lakes, a collaboration of four full-member institutions and sixteen affiliated colleges and universities, operates a campus in the Bahamas where students and faculty members research environmental issues. This consortium also has a 65-foot vessel that plies Seneca Lake in upper New York State, providing a floating environmental studies laboratory. The Central Pennsylvania Consortium, founded in 1967 by Dickinson, Franklin and Marshall, Gettysburg, and Wilson colleges, directed its early efforts to off-campus study programs. The three initial joint activities included an urban semester in Harrisburg, the state capital, a program in India at the University of Mysore, and a Latin American seminar offered in conjunction with the University of Bolivar in Medellin, Colombia. All are open to qualified students from both within and without the consortium (Patterson, 1975). These programs are typical of the kinds of activities that smaller colleges may do in consort but may find impossible to do alone.

A variation on this kind of consortium involves the collaboration of a nonacademic institution with groups of colleges and universities. This alternative to strictly college-based consortia is slowly emerging as museums, libraries, and other educational institutions are building bridges to the collegiate sector. These institutions are proving that they can greatly enhance the varieties of education offered on campuses at relatively little cost; sometimes they even take the lead in establishing cooperative ventures. An unusual example of this kind of special purpose collaboration involves a zoo and three colleges.

In recent years, the Oregon Zoological Research Center, better known as the Portland Zoo, has developed an extensive basic research program focusing on animal behavior and physiology. Believing that students from local colleges could benefit from participating in these research activities, zoo officials approached a number of schools to explore various forms of cooperation. In 1977, the zoo concluded a formal arrangement with Whitman and Reed colleges and Portland State University to enable their students to receive academic credit for work as voluntary research assistants at the zoo. In the fall of 1978, courses in animal behavior, including a research practicum, were taught by zoo staff members as part of the regular course offerings of two participating colleges, while more than one hundred students became involved in the zoo's research activities (Fund for the Improvement of Postsecondary Education, 1977).

Another example representing more than simply a collaboration of colleges and universities is the Rochester/Genesee Valley History Project in New York State, which involves community agencies, museums, the local media, and colleges and universities in teaching local history. Students from participating schools can select from among a variety of off-campus learning activities, including oral history projects, historical preservation work, archival studies, photographic exhibits, and the production of radio and television programs. Since this effort focuses on community history, the consortium also provides programs for individuals not currently enrolled in any particular school.

Surely one of the most comprehensive consortia, offering students the widest possible range of both on- and off-campus learn-

45

ing options, is the Worcester Consortium for Higher Education (WCHE) in Massachusetts. In addition to a dozen colleges and universities, WCHE also encompasses many types of educational organizations, including the American Antiquarian Society, Old Sturbridge Village, the Worcester Art Museum, and the Worcester County Horticultural Society. Not only can students cross-register for courses at the collaborating colleges, they can also take part in a number of programs (for credit and noncredit) offered at noncollegiate learning sites (Patterson, 1975).

Despite the obvious advantages of consortia that are not strictly collegiate, few schools have fully embraced their sister educational organizations and vice versa. Even when a museum is adjacent to a college, it has proven difficult to get these institutions to cooperate on programs and procedures beyond an occasional joint exhibit or lecture series. Part of the problem lies with the closed nature of the academic enterprise. Faculty members are frequently unwilling to award credit to students who pursue courses of study off campus and under the direction of "lay" experts. In retaliation, museum curators or archivists do not readily share their facilities and resources with persons from the collegiate sector. Unfortunately, as long as these turf issues remain unresolved, students will continue to be the big losers. Ultimately, however, small institutions will also suffer, since interinstitutional arrangements of this type are likely to strengthen a college's ability to attract and hold undergraduates.

Recommendations

Without minimizing the difficulties involved in creating successful collaborations, we believe that smaller institutions should seize the opportunity to strengthen themselves through cooperation. In this way, they can provide more diversity in courses and curriculum to students without changing the nature of their academic programs or their scale of operation. We have suggested that the most common forms of collaboration may not necessarily enhance the learning options that any one school already offers. Institutions wishing to broaden their involvement with other schools should consider the following list of checkpoints:

46

Increasing Learning Options Without Expansion

1. What courses and curriculums can another institution provide that students are now not receiving?
2. How similar are the institution's procedures—calendar, course schedules, grading systems?
3. What kind of "intensive" cooperation is desirable—cross-registration, joint-degree programs, internship opportunities?
4. What kinds of learning sites already exist in close proximity— museums, libraries, industries?
5. What kinds of new programs would your institution like to mount if it had the financial resources?

Beyond these questions about the value of cooperation lies the more troubling problem of making these cooperative ventures work. A good deal has been written about the failure of collaborations to deliver economic and educational benefits (Quehl, 1972). As the Carnegie Commission (1971, p. 93) remarks, "Despite the promise in the consortia movement, many existing consortia are largely arrangements on paper that have little actual impact." We are not urging smaller institutions to jump on the consortia bandwagon as a panacea. Rather, we suggest that new forms of interinstitutional collaboration can yield significant benefits to learners in small colleges. When Franklin Patterson (1974) wrote *Colleges in Consort,* he singled out five varieties for special study. None of those consortia included noncollegiate institutions, and only one, the Union of Independent Colleges of Art, served a specialized purpose.

The cooperative arrangements described in this chapter push the concept of consortia beyond traditional boundaries, creating new links between learning and work sites and vocational and liberal education. We believe that these unlikely collaborations may well enrich students' collegiate experiences more than traditional consortia. We urge college administrators to think *small* about entering into collaborations that are focused on particular educational goals but to stretch their imaginations to think *boldly* about the range of educational goals that might be enhanced through collaborations without increasing size.

47

CHAPTER FOUR

Shrinking Scale by New Cluster Colleges

A shallow creek runs a few hundred yards on the University of California's Berkeley campus from Bancroft Library along a cluster of trees to a narrow green wooden building that looks remarkably like a movie set of a World War II army barracks. Instead of housing GIs, this building contains the Collegiate Seminar Program, better known as Strawberry Creek College. Strawberry Creek is the latest and seemingly most successful attempt to create an undergraduate cluster college at this university. After four years, the college, with four full-time faculty members and 100 students, is beginning to have an impact both at Berkeley and beyond the University of California (UC) system quite out of proportion to its small size. The strength and impact of the program derives from

49

its modest scale; its explicit goal is the creation of a manageable learning environment within a massive educational institution.

Strawberry Creek is one of a number of modest experiments that are seeking to humanize large universities by developing new variations on the concept of the cluster college. Although hardly a fresh educational reform, this idea has caught the imagination of innovators in the 1970s as it did in the 1960s. Now this concept is being used primarily to achieve the benefits of small scale within large units; reformers are making no pretense about providing the coherent liberal arts curriculum that cluster colleges were conceived to deliver a decade ago.

During the 1960s, educators who were moved by student protests and wished to reform the quality of undergraduate instruction seized the idea of cluster colleges as a means of revitalizing the curriculum. These were the colleges that Jerry Gaff (1970, p. 16) defined as "semiautonomous schools on the campus of a larger institution which share, to a significant extent, facilities and services with the other schools." In 1969 in California alone, eight institutions were implementing or actively planning a cluster college structure. The college could be as small as a hundred students or, as in the case of the federated colleges of the Atlanta University complex, the concept could accommodate five institutions, some with enrollments of more than a thousand students each. The similarity between these examples obviously is not their absolute size but rather their relative size as compared with the massiveness of the total enterprise. Generally, smaller cluster colleges were found in private institutions, while higher enrollments characterized cluster colleges in public universities. Also, these semiautonomous programs usually, but not always, offered some kind of degree program.

Cluster Colleges of the 1960s

The cluster college movement was originally seen as an answer to the fragmentation of undergraduate education in both large and small universities. Many academics were distressed by the listing of a staggering 10,000 courses at UC Berkeley; but almost as startling was the fact that Stanford, a small university, listed a total of 523 different undergraduate courses in four disciplines—philosophy, history, English, and political science—in a recent catalogue. Thus it is not surprising that cluster college models in the late 1960s and 1970s emphasized the core curriculum. These colleges were supposed to bring coherence to lower-division collegiate work. As one cluster college professor remarked, the purpose of his college was to provide an "integrated education in an intellectually disintegrated world"—a difficult assignment. Yet many faculty members and administrators had this concept in mind when they implemented their own versions of the complete curriculum. Before Strawberry Creek, Berkeley had Tussman College, a typical 1960s cluster college.

Tussman College was established by Joseph Tussman, a faculty member, following the 1964 Free Speech controversy at Berkeley. It offered a two-year interdisciplinary program to a small group of liberal arts majors; the core curriculum focused on intellectual issues in Western thought and had its roots in the "Great Books" approach pioneered at the University of Chicago under Robert Hutchins. At first, students flocked to the program and junior faculty members seemed interested. Within three years, however, Tussman College faltered and collapsed.

Why did the college fail? Most observers agree that the unwillingness of the senior faculty to participate and support the program was a crucial factor in its demise. Since it did not offer a four-year program, Tussman was not a pure cluster college, and it threw its sophomore generalists into an alien pool of specialists for the remaining years of their undergraduate education. The generalists were overwhelmed by and unprepared for the decisions they would have to make concerning courses, professional education, and careers. Other criticisms leveled at the college included inadequate administration, permissiveness, and exorbitant costs. Some cynics even suggested that the college was a political symbol, serving more as a safety valve that appeared to promise real reform than as a radical departure from Berkeley's past educational practices. By the late 1960s, students had lost interest in the Tussman model.

51

The Tussman experience reflected the concerns of and problems faced by other cluster colleges. Bensalem College at Fordham University, in New York City, and Monteith College at Wayne University, in Detroit, also tried to combat student criticisms of the educational enterprise by developing special curricular programs. All three colleges, despite differences in structuring and packaging, were moving toward a definition of a coherent liberal arts education. They attracted students with high aspirations, good grades, and general disillusionment with the standard curriculum because it lacked either coherence or relevance or both. The students who chose these programs were academically, rather than vocationally, oriented and often represented the best and the brightest from among the larger student pool. In the rarified atmosphere of such a college, where, as in the case of Bensalem, teachers and students not only studied together, but lived together, much learning occurred. All students received extraordinary attention, and some blossomed intellectually, while others found new causes for disaffection with the academic enterprise.

Because of their political origins, the kinds of students they attracted, and their general mission, cluster colleges seemed a poor risk. A handful of them started in the late 1960s have survived, but most lost out in the financial squeezes of the 1970s. Internal squabbles between faculty members and students also forced some to close prematurely. The Residential College at the University of Michigan is surviving on external funding and is deliberately trying to be as unthreatening to the university as possible. To survive, the college requires considerable financial backing and heavy faculty involvement, while it benefits only a small percentage of the student population. Small wonder then that decision makers have viewed the cluster college as a costly addition that may enhance some students' experiences but often tears the larger institution and itself apart.

The notion of introducing a cluster college concept in a rapidly growing, massive, nonselective institution that catered to a heterogeneous, nonresidential student population seemed the worst folly. Yet it was increasingly apparent that the students who could benefit most from smallness and cluster colleges were precisely those

Shrinking Scale by New Cluster Colleges

students in the new public universities and colleges, which offered little in the way of a residential community. Their students suffered from a lack of integration with the academic world. Unlike their predecessors, the new, or nontraditional, students have problems with academe stemming less from a sense of disjointedness with "real" world concerns than from a sense of separateness from the collegiate life. Whereas the students who flocked to Tussman and Bensalem might have been better served by having less interaction with school and a chance to work in the real world, new students need a greater opportunity for interaction and contact with faculty members and a chance to immerse themselves in student life. Until recently, the option has not been widely available.

Cluster Colleges of the 1970s

Despite the problems of cluster colleges in the past, a few institutions are now experimenting with variations of the model. The experiments are not confined strictly to a residential collegiate setting; the concept has been broadened to emphasize the clustering of courses and people instead of the development of a total curriculum. New "clusters" can be found in established institutions such as UC Berkeley and also in newly formed universities, such as the State University of New York (SUNY) at Stony Brook, which cater to commuting students over twenty-one years old as well as to a residential, younger student group. New clusters are not exclusively designed for one special population selected or self-selected on the basis of the student's interest in a core curriculum. Avoiding rhetoric that tells students they will receive a holistic liberal education, the programs assert that within each cluster, regardless of the content, students will learn to use the tools for mastering a variety of subjects. Hence, there is no fixed curriculum, immutable from year to year. The programs develop a fluid cluster of courses and experiences, which may change from semester to semester. In short, the cluster college model is still alive but it is being transformed and tested in new settings with different kinds of students. Gone is the promise of the core curriculum that guarantees students a complete liberal arts education. In its place is the more realistic cluster college that serves as an antidote to the problems of massiveness. Let us take a closer look here at a few recent experiments to see how they differ from earlier examples and how they are doing.

In 1976, SUNY at Stony Brook and the University of Maryland at Baltimore County (UMBC) inaugurated cluster college projects. Stony Brook dubbed its experiment "the Federated Courses" approach and UMBC christened its effort "the Freshman Cluster." The institutions are alike in many respects and developed these programs in response to similar needs. Both institutions are branch campuses of a larger university system—Stony Brook, with its graduate and professional schools, is a university center, sixty miles from New York City and more than two hundred miles from SUNY's central administration in Albany; UMBC is an addition to the University of Maryland system, which has its central office at College Park, twenty-five miles from the campus. Both institutions are less than twenty years old and grew up alongside suburban bedroom communities and transplanted industries that left the cities. Their student bodies are diverse—they enroll freshmen directly out of high school plus a sizable number of older students. The majority of the students attend full time and hold a part-time or full-time job in addition. Both campuses attract some minority students, although the commuting problems make it difficult for inner-city students to carry a full load of courses. Both Stony Brook and UMBC grew rapidly in the 1970s, and this growth led ineluctably to the kinds of learner-centered problems encountered in large institutions: students felt no sense of community; they complained of a lack of attention; their course work seemed disconnected from their educational goals; and some just felt overwhelmed by the total experience. As a result, attrition rates were high at both institutions, and those who stayed honestly questioned the value of the learning experience and the institution's academic integrity; student disaffection took the form of malaise rather than protest. Both institutions responded with the cluster college model.

The core of the Federated Course approach at Stony Brook is the development of a community rather than a new curriculum.

Shrinking Scale by New Cluster Colleges

As Patrick Hill, a professor of philosophy and originator of the Stony Brook model, explains, "The purpose of this experiment is the revitalization of the institution through the birth (or rebirth) of academic community" (1976, p. 5). The generation of a community, Hill contends, is still possible within the large impersonal university without a radical change in the teaching styles or scholarship goals of the faculty. The key is the way in which courses in the program are *federated*: a theme is chosen and three regularly scheduled courses are linked together as a program. Professors from each course will emphasize the theme as it relates to their own disciplines. In one sense, then, the program is not interdisciplinary because faculty members are not asked to significantly alter the curriculum to cover material from other disciplines. Instead, the integrating function is performed by a fourth faculty member—the master learner, who attends all classes and then presides over a program seminar in which themes from each course are discussed and compared. The faculty members also meet throughout the semester to share information on students and swap curriculum ideas.

In this model, much of the responsibility for the generation of a community rests on the expertise and involvement of the master learner. The individual in this role must serve as a mentor, promote learning, and be familiar with subject matter outside his or her own discipline. "In the span of the program," Hill (1976, p. 12) writes, "the master learner's presence as a student in the classroom with other students enables him to assist students to integrate the perspectives of the various disciplines in courses."

In its first year of operation, the federated learning program deliberately sought tenured teachers and received an encouraging response. Faculty applications exceeded the number of openings, and eventually two federated programs were started. Courses from the biology, sociology, philosophy, economics, English, and political science departments were federated under the theme of "World Hunger." Students could elect a maximum of three federated courses each semester, although most chose to take a total of four federated classes for the entire year.

In addition to the master learner, the Stony Brook model

builds community in a number of indirect ways. Professors have an opportunity to learn from one another and break down discipline-based barriers. Students begin to see faculty members as learners as well as teachers. Problems with the courses can be raised in the seminar with the master learner, who then brings those problems back to her colleagues. Students in federated courses develop friendships through increased association. And, finally, the master learner's seminar serves as a formal after-class rap session. Building this aspect of interaction into the Stony Brook curriculum is an ingenious way of ensuring that students have an opportunity to share their educational experiences with one another.

Although it just began in 1976, the program at Stony Brook holds much promise and deserves close scrutiny. Hill and his colleagues hope to develop ten federated programs by 1980 without the infusion of large sums of money, believing that this model, which builds so heavily on already existing courses and faculty members, will counter charges that cluster colleges are not cost effective. Hill (1976, p. 13) describes this strategy: "It is mainstream in that it accepts already existing departmentally based courses in research interests as the fundamental building blocks of the university education. It is radical in that it creates a structure in which those courses and skills function to a radically different end, which addresses the problems of fragmentation and impersonality."

The University of Maryland at Baltimore County articulated a number of problem areas in its 1975 self-study conducted in conjunction with an accreditation evaluation. Students were having trouble taking advantage of the campus educational resources—they were not studying. Yet many were not flunking out—they were leaving. This phenomenon led the faculty and administration to identify freshman attrition as the most serious shortcoming of the institution (University of Maryland . . . , 1975). The task force report on problems at UMBC speculated that since 82 percent of all students were commuting and 66 percent were employed, it was hard to find, let alone tutor or counsel, students to help them adjust to the expectations of the university. "Students spend minimal time on campus and participate minimally in the academic community," óne administrator commented (Alexander, 1976, p. 10). Certainly it was difficult to sort out the causes of attrition, but that difficulty did not justify simply dismissing students as unprepared for college-level work.

The task force report recommended the development of a nine-credit freshman cluster college curriculum. Each cluster would have a theme, but the curriculum would not presume to cover the first year of a student's entire liberal arts, or breadth, requirement. Instead, teams of faculty members would work together to reinforce study skills, reading and writing competence, and the "development of the intellectual skills of inquiry, analysis, and expression" (1975, p. 9). Unlike the Stony Brook model, the UMBC plan called for the transformation of courses to emphasize the acquisition of learning skills. Also, the faculty was expected to introduce students into the world of academe by focusing on affective as well as cognitive issues in learning, such as forming values, improving self-image and interpersonal skills, and focusing on career aspirations. Two freshman clusters were to be pilot programs in 1976, with faculty members and counselors randomly assigning students to each cluster. The faculty planning team hoped that eventually all freshman students would be required to take a cluster upon entering the college.

The UMBC experiment attracted younger faculty members, but it did not generate the kind of enthusiasm that greeted the Stony Brook program. Because of the nature of the courses to be taught, many tenured faculty members were not interested in the curriculum development aspects of the project. In addition, shortly after the program received outside funding, the chancellor resigned. Support from the administration weakened, and communication between campus groups responsible for curriculum policies suffered.

Senior faculty members criticized the program during the planning stage; they were suspicious about it even though many agreed with the task force's recommendation. They challenged the competence of the project leadership, expressed concern over the quality of the courses, and ultimately succeeded in eliminating those aspects of the curriculum that dealt explicitly with affective issues and student development. Their common complaint was that the

57

freshman cluster would be paying too much attention to basic skills and counseling and too little to knowledge acquisition.

Nevertheless, the college began two clusters in the fall semester of 1976. Students were assigned to the program, and most agreed to participate in the pilot testing. One cluster program dealt with urban studies and the other with development in third world countries; they were taught by junior faculty members, two thirds of whom were nontenured. Preliminary evaluations disclosed that both the students and faculty felt the program was a success and an improvement over the typical curriculum offered to freshmen at UMBC. Since classes were block scheduled—that is, one group of students took several classes together—a team of faculty members could follow students' progress and learning rather than merely record attendance. Program faculty members reported that they appreciated the increased contact with students and the opportunity to share views with other teachers. Although the program was labor intensive—they spent more time counseling students than usual—the program faculty members were more satisfied with their teaching as a result.

In spite of this early evidence that the program had promise, it was disbanded for the 1977–78 academic year. Few new faculty members were willing to volunteer to work in it. The cluster programs had the reputation of being a drain on faculty time, and there were no incentives and rewards for participating. Until basic skills education at UMBC is deemed as significant as teaching advanced courses in a discipline, it appears that regular faculty members will not devote their energies to this kind of freshman education even if all agree that it is a pressing need. Looking back over the development of the UMBC model, we see that the freshman cluster never had the serious support of the tenured faculty, and it lost whatever support it was able to generate by emphasizing developmental issues in undergraduate education.

Strawberry Creek College at Berkeley is also actively concerned with the development of students' skills, although this concern is not publicized. Unlike UMBC, Strawberry Creek College did not make a frontal attack on the basic skills issue. In fact, Strawberry Creek did not claim to offer an organized curriculum in any traditional sense. It was neither a thematic college nor a basic skills cluster. Like both SUNY at Stony Brook and UMBC, Strawberry Creek was created to improve students' learning experiences in the freshman and sophomore years. But that is where the similarities end.

Strawberry Creek College is organized around the research interests of the senior faculty members who teach in it. As Charles Muscatine, the originator of the college and author of the influential 1966 *Muscatine Report* on general education, observes, "Faculty teach their next book." Courses are offered in the form of small, interdisciplinary research seminars, which meet for a total of six hours weekly but carry nine credits. They are jointly led by faculty members and graduate students from different departments. During one semester Strawberry Creek offered such courses as "Comparative Revolutions," "The Food Crisis," and "Formation of Roles of Men and Women in Western Culture." Students write short research papers each week throughout the semester, and the in-class work also emphasizes writing as well as the analysis of primary documents. In short, Strawberry Creek College reverses the usual progression of undergraduate education. Instead of assigning freshmen to large survey courses, Strawberry Creek immerses students directly in research and investigation.

In 1975, after one year of operation, evaluations of Strawberry Creek College indicated that the program was especially effective with students who had writing deficiencies. Approximately twenty out of the one hundred students enrolled in the program had failed the "bonehead" English placement examination, which is given to all incoming Berkeley freshmen. Muscatine succeeded in bending university policy so that the freshmen who had failed the examination were permitted to take a Strawberry Creek seminar in lieu of a remedial English class. Since all students in the program, regardless of their levels of proficiency, must write weekly papers, students with deficiencies received personal attention. By the end of the semester, fifteen of the twenty students who had originally failed the examination passed it. Berkeley freshmen enrolled in so-called remedial classes had a lower passing rate than those who were integrated in the collegiate seminar program of Strawberry Creek.

One key to the college's success with underprepared students at Berkeley may lie precisely in the fact that the students deficient in writing were not treated differently, isolated, or tracked into demeaning courses. If the UMBC model had been applied across the board for all students, perhaps the stigma of participating in "remedial" clusters would have lifted. Muscatine's goal for Strawberry Creek is no different from that expressed by the UMBC task force—the development of intellectual skills. However, Muscatine chose to focus on different means to achieve the same ends; the means are research-based classes, which do not contradict faculty members' self-interests. In fact, students are introduced into the life of the scholar in fresh and compelling ways that directly help them make sense of the institution's purpose. "Instead of surveying a broad area of received knowledge," Muscatine (1973, p. 30) writes, "each seminar, by focusing on a relatively new and unexplored problem, enables the student to learn the methods of investigation."

Not surprisingly, this research and investigative approach has won many converts among the tenured faculty at UC Berkeley. All five of the teachers in 1976 were full professors. These faculty members have vigorously defended the program to other professors and administrators as a successful way to address the plight of both students and teachers who wish to feel less alienated from each other and from the institution (Maeroff, 1976; Trombley, 1975).

It has been said that the large scale of research-oriented universities separates the faculty and students and that nothing can be done about it. At the State University of New York at Buffalo, for example, students must take buses between the language buildings and the science complex, located on the same campus but miles apart. Departments remain isolated, and the faculty teaching on the graduate level often has little contact with undergraduate education. Even the architecture of institutions, Muscatine (1973, p. 1) points out, "threatens to freeze education in patterns worked out decades ago." Strawberry Creek College challenges the rigidities of both buildings and academic conventions. It is no accident that the college has taken over a ramshackle site in the center of the campus where students and faculty can gather. Muscatine was quite willing to sacrifice appearance for the common space that gave these diverse persons a sense of community. They do not study the same material, but they are all committed to the investigative method and the creation of academic community.

Obviously, one must be careful about extolling diversity at Berkeley or even within Strawberry Creek College. Compared to that of the City University of New York or a sprawling community College, Strawberry Creek's student body hardly seems heterogeneous. But when one compares them with students at other more traditional cluster colleges, one can detect a greater degree of interaction among students planning majors in liberal arts, medicine, engineering, and business. In fact, one obstacle to student participation in Strawberry Creek's Collegiate Seminar Program has been the fact that departments begin recruiting quite early, urging students to enroll in certain sequences of required courses. Students at Strawberry Creek are torn between wanting to take a freshman-sophomore program in the college and recognizing the pressure to begin specialization.

The phenomenon of students choosing depth over breadth is widespread and has its roots in a number of changes in higher education during the past ten years. The Carnegie Council's report (Blackburn and others, 1976) on these changes comments on factors that have propelled students into majors almost immediately upon arrival at college. One is the elimination of general education requirements because of the faculty's unwillingness to take responsibility for knowing what constitutes an educated person. (We have come a long way from the prescriptive core curriculums of the 1960s.) But more important, the council noted that although faculty members did not want to be accountable for general education, they assert that they know what is required to become a specialist in a field or profession. In short, while required courses in liberal learning have been diminishing, requirements for a major have been

The Impersonal Campus

maintained and in some instances increased. Also, the competition has become so stiff in certain professional fields that students are convinced it is advantageous to declare majors early and take everything the department has to offer, thereby impressing the faculty with their serious commitment to the profession.

As a response to this trend toward specialization, some colleges have reinstituted required general education courses and have returned to the concept of distributing requirements among disciplines. One limitation of this approach is that distribution requirements have never guaranteed that students will emerge from college liberally educated. But, more significant, such a structural requirement only sidesteps the real question of what determines an educated person. A return to distribution requirements in a massive institution may also have deleterious effects on attempts to create community. At least students who specialize early come to know their teachers and fellow students interested in the same subject matter more intimately over a longer time. In fact, overspecialization with a structurally fragmented approach to liberal learning may not accomplish the breadth purposes of the curriculum and could exacerbate students' sense of alienation from the institution.

Strawberry Creek College has struggled with the problem of overspecialization and is proposing an alternative to the reestablishment of distribution requirements. It has just won approval to award the bachelor's degree. This hardly seems revolutionary, since cluster colleges have offered their own independent degrees in the past. For example, Berkeley's sister campus, Santa Cruz, consists of eight colleges, each with particular degree requirements in addition to the required courses prescribed by departments, the discipline-based Boards of Study. The unusual feature of the Strawberry Creek B.A. degree will be the *lack* of a required course curriculum. There are no distribution requirements, and students do not elect to major in a discipline. Instead, they must take a certain number of Strawberry Creek seminars, participate in an "integrating" senior seminar, and spend their junior year working on a particular project, which can incorporate research, experiential learning, or creative expression in the arts. The junior year project is determined in conjunction with a faculty member and bears a striking resemblance to the Oxford and Cambridge tutorial system. The project can take almost any form—a paper, a film, work in a social action agency, even cooperative research among a group of students. The fourth or final year of the Strawberry Creek degree program is devoted to synthesizing experiences, skills, and insights. By then, students have already completed their major project and can reflect on their accumulated knowledge and experience through discussions and theoretical papers. Once again, the program reverses the typical progression of academic work—group discussions *follow* independent work; thus, rather than ending with a quasi-thesis executed in isolation, the undergraduate program closes with cooperative communication.

How will students and the faculty at UC Berkeley respond to this new baccalaureate degree? Planners at the college believe they can interest students in completing most of their undergraduate education at Strawberry Creek without reducing their chances for acceptance into professional and graduate school programs. The Strawberry Creek degree will constitute 60 percent of the student's course work, allowing the individual to elect necessary discipline-based courses. It is unclear whether faculty members who have been generally supportive of the program during its first three years of operation will continue their support, especially when Strawberry Creek offers a four-year alternative to the departmentally based Berkeley curriculum. Will departments allow "Strawberries" to enroll in advanced courses as electives? Will the faculty see the cluster college as a growing threat to their own departments' enrollments? Muscatine has tried to allay fears by emphasizing the smallness of the operation. He does not envisage more than one hundred B.A. candidates at any one time. But if the program catches on, how can Muscatine turn students away? The Fund for the Improvement of Postsecondary Education has supported Strawberry Creek College through its first years of development, and support for another three years has just been pledged by the Berkeley administration. However, as the college attracts new students away from other disciplines, Muscatine may find his coalition of administrators and tenured faculty beginning to disintegrate. Of the three models described in this chapter, Strawberry Creek has the longest record of support and appears to have the strongest chances of survival, but its future is not certain.

Despite their differences, the three models described in this chapter are a far cry from the cluster colleges of the 1960s. They reject the task of deciding on and exposing students to "The Curriculum." Faculty members are not set on transmitting information on specific subjects. The colleges have replaced a core curriculum with a core purpose—the creation and encouragement of a learning community. The purpose reflects the belief that the primary prerequisite for learning is an environment that promotes and nurtures inquiry, critical thinking, intellectual honesty, and mutual respect among students and faculty members. These, we would argue, are the attributes of a meaningful college education that are being undermined in massive institutions. The cluster colleges are deliberately small, have low faculty-student ratios (which also translate in these settings into more faculty-student interaction), and built-in opportunities for group discussions. These characteristics are a break from the assembly-line educational techniques commonly found in the undergraduate programs of large, research-oriented universities. New cluster colleges are signaling important changes in the ways educators organize learning settings and teach the skills they hope students will acquire. But we are aware that a few models hardly constitute a major trend. If administrators and faculties are unwilling to experiment with these approaches, we must find out what, if anything, they are doing about the negative consequences of the bigger is better syndrome.

CHAPTER FIVE

Modest Ways to Overcome Massiveness

In the foreseeable future, it is difficult to imagine that colleges and universities will, like Alice in Lewis Carroll's *Through the Looking Glass,* suddenly shrink to one-tenth their size. Massive institutions will be around for a long time, and a majority of students will be attending them primarily because they cannot afford to go anywhere else. A major concern then is how can these schools be made more manageable and humane places? This chapter attempts to answer that question. We owe it to students attending colleges with enrollments in excess of ten thousand, particularly commuter colleges, to scrutinize our policies and determine as best we can, in the absence of the definitive research report, whether our practices promote or obstruct the creation of small learning communities. The task is not simple.

Although it is relatively easy to uncover those aspects of institutional life that need changing, a problem arises over finding an appropriate alternative practice. Often innovators implement a new program because on paper it appears to be a solution to a perceived problem. They later discover that the innovation has produced altered patterns within the university that ultimately work against their original goals. Inappropriate strategies may have hampered efforts to offset mass massiveness. Few educators explicitly claimed, for example, that individualized instruction, consumer education, and increased counseling and support services were developed solely for the purpose of combating the negative effects of large, impersonal schools. But during the past decade, these are the practices that, in fact, have been most commonly employed by administrators and faculties wishing to prove that they are doing something. Here we will first look at these three approaches to see how they are being used and whether they are contributing to a solution or merely exacerbating the problems of fragmentation and overspecialization often associated with massive institutions. Then we will turn to some other possible responses, which appear less radical and comprehensive but may in the long run prove as useful or more useful in helping to establish a sense of small scale within large institutions.

Individualized Instruction

Individualized instruction is an umbrella phrase covering a variety of educational programs. Under this rubric we include the personalized system of instruction (PSI), computer assisted instruction (CAI), programmed instruction, auto-tutorial instruction (A-TI), mastery learning, and self-paced instruction. K. Patricia Cross (1976), in her survey of the instructional revolution, *Accent on Learning,* provides a thorough analysis of the characteristics of these learning processes.

We have lumped these programs together because they all follow one basic theme: They package and organize the transmis-

66

sion of information in a way that permits students to master the material at their own pace, assisted by some combination of faculty, peer tutors, or machines. Each program emphasizes the concept that students must take responsibility for learning, and so individualized instruction means self-directed education. Because it does not require any particular form of instruction, we have not included contract learning, in which students sign contracts indicating what they hope to learn during a given time. Even the most rigorous individualized program does not rely exclusively on one method of learning, and hence there is no single, pure model. But for the purposes of our analysis, individualized instruction can be readily distinguished from the conventional classroom and course syllabus format. And even its harshest critics and strongest supporters agree that all individualized instruction is an attempt to shift the primary responsibility for the teaching-learning process from the teachers to the students to ensure that the students learn the material regardless of the quality of the teaching.

Individualized instruction in all its myriad forms emerged as a major force in higher education just as colleges and universities were opening their doors to the masses. As Cross (1976, p. 11) notes, "Ironically, the influx of large numbers of new students into colleges has brought about the individualization of instruction." The simultaneous occurrence of these two events was not accidental. Colleges and universities faced with overwhelming numbers and new demands found that individualized instruction was a way to provide education that promised reduced instructional costs and more effective use of resources. In addition, administrators and faculty members discovered sound educational reasons for turning to individualized instruction.

While the material to be mastered remained a constant, this system recognized individual differences in the ways in which people learn and the rate at which they assimilate new information. Furthermore, individualized instruction demanded a different kind of accountability from teachers. They had to make the learning objectives of their curriculum precise and explicit, but they were freed from the obligation of being responsible for students' performance.

67

Students had to master material as they went along; they could not just cram for a final examination, and they could not blame teachers for their lack of progress.

Individualized instruction also presented many advantages from the student's point of view. Courses were broken down into manageable learning units. Each unit incorporated specific goals, and students always knew what was expected of them. They received immediate feedback concerning progress, and the only penalty for failure was loss of time. Individualized instruction promised students personal attention, although, in fact, the inflexibility of the curricular units suggests that much of what was rhetorically described as individualized really meant packaged.

Reports from the field and evaluations have indicated that individualized instructional programs have won converts and are proving themselves effective in specific settings. Research on the use of PSI and CAI shows that faculty members are employing these techniques to teach math and science in biology, physics, engineering, and psychology. The Center for Personalized Instruction at Georgetown University reports that there are approximately eight hundred self-paced courses in psychology alone (Cross, 1976, p. 93). A 1974 survey by Cross (1976) revealed that nearly three fourths of American community colleges reported some use of self-paced learning modules. Students appear to react favorably to CAI, for example, especially when they realize they will not be graded in a traditional manner. Women at the University of Minnesota preferred to be tutored by a computer than by a male professor in calculus. It was less threatening to try out a possibly "dumb" question on a machine than risk embarrassment with a teacher or classmates. Students who expect to do poorly in a conventional class are optimistic about the chances of improving performance in a personalized learning program. Many educators urge individualized instruction as a means to aid academically deficient students, noting that these students suffer from being compared with others in a traditional classroom. Such students, they assert, need highly structured learning processes to understand what is expected of them. Since individualized instruction is based on a system of positive reinforcement, there are no lasting penalties for wrong answers. It is, in short, a more humane way to reward merit. Students can succeed academically because they are not constrained by time, previous preparation, or the impatience of their fellow classmates. Or so the argument goes.

However, one could make the opposite case. We ought to be cautious about using individualized instruction with academically deficient students, especially in large, anonymous, and impersonal situations. Students who have seldom experienced the intrinsic satisfactions of self-generated learning are the last ones on which to lay open-ended, teacherless mastery learning. These students may need personalized attention, but they also deserve the experience of success in traditional courses. In addition, the computer, even with highly sophisticated programs for moving students through skills exercises, may not be able to detect the kinds of error patterns that informed teachers can quickly discover. The computer cannot analyze the reasons behind wrong responses beyond making a crude guess based on the minimal information the response itself provides. The sight of a laboratory in which scores of remedial students are plugged into auto-tutorial earphones or typing out drills on a computer terminal disturbs faculty members who believe that low-achieving students should have the opportunity to learn in a variety of settings. They argue that there is little self-direction in this kind of individualized instruction.

Also, some teachers are troubled by the political implications underlying the wholesale adaptation of individualized instruction at the remedial level. Although it may be true that some low achievers learn basic skills through the individualized programs, they wonder whether this achievement is worth the price of further distinguishing these students from more traditionally successful learners. It is, at best, a Pyrrhic victory if this learning system only reinforces the stigma of difference between the academically competent student and the high-risk student. What are the trade-offs involved in implementing an individualized approach to basic skills education? Are these trade-offs different depending on the size of an institution?

High-risk students need to interact with peers, to discuss

ideas and challenge one another intellectually, to grow into the world of academe, to develop as conscious learners. Much individualized instruction assumes that these affective dimensions are covered elsewhere in the curriculum. But massive institutions do not provide alternative structures or practices. The virtues of individualized instruction may be better suited to advanced learners in residential settings who have mastered the skills of studenthood. This conclusion is borne out by evidence on the effectiveness of personalized systems of instruction, which indicates that it works especially well with students who are above average in academic achievement (Sherman, 1974; Robin, 1976).

Another issue to be considered in weighing the efficacy of individualized instruction is its tendency to further fragment a student's perception of the curriculum. Mastering units or modules in the absence of an overarching integrative learning experience and the chance to share insights with others may leave students even more cut off from the purposes of their education than they were when they attended traditional classes. At least classes provide an arbitrary community of persons all struggling to make sense out of similar material. In a curriculum wholly designed for one individual, such as contract learning, or packaged in such a way that thirty persons may be studying thirty different units, there is no external reference point for the student. Individualized instruction can be a lonely way to get an education; it suggests the nightmare vision of students receiving their education in measured moments while buzzing through college in single-seat, self-contained learning vehicles equipped with earphones, microphones, and instant replays of their responses. Since individualized instruction focuses exclusively on cognitive development as opposed to affective growth, we must be careful not to let individualized instruction exacerbate our present inadequacies in educating the whole person (see Smith, 1974).

Many of these concerns are less serious when individualized instruction is offered in small residence colleges as one teaching-learning strategy among many. Students have a variety of ways to establish contact and to grow in interpersonal relations while taking a PSI psychology course alongside a standard history seminar. We believe the negative effects of individualized instruction have a considerably greater impact in just those institutions that are touting the model and appear less well equipped to balance this process with other learning activities.

Some disturbing signs are leading us to rethink whether individualized instruction is an appropriate strategy to reduce the problem of massiveness in higher education. One sign is that students are bored; they are not behaving as the behavioral learning theorists said they would. They are becoming disinterested in the modularized approach and are not making much progress through the semester's curriculum. College IV, the self-paced college in the Grand Valley State Colleges system in Michigan, reports that many students who elect an individualized program have a poor completion rate. They do not finish the module, or they tend to put off work until the end of the semester when they are busy studying for conventional final examinations (Toft, 1975). To increase motivation, the faculty at Grand Valley is proposing letter grades rather than the typical mastery/no mastery evaluation. In a recent survey concerning PSI utilization, 71 percent of the faculty members responding noted that they had problems with student apathy and procrastination (Cross, 1976, p. 100).

Few educators have questioned the view that individualized instruction is a way to break down the anonymity of huge lecture classes. For example, it is generally held that "the advantages of auto-tutorial education are undoubtedly greater for large classes than for small" (Cross, 1976, p. 88). But we wonder whether this is an accurate perception. The A-TI method was conceived in 1961 by Samuel Postlethwait as a response to the problems of teaching four hundred students introductory biology at Purdue University. The lecture method was inadequate, according to Postlethwait, because students could not keep up with the material and the teacher did not know which students were having difficulty. In desperation, he developed the A-TI method.

In auto-tutorial instruction, a student is directed to engage in certain learning activities by the faculty member via a tape that is audio or audiovisual. These activities may include reading, lab-

71

oratory work, film and slide presentations, and research assignments. Students receive directives in an independent study center, which remains open throughout the day and evening. Once a week, students gather for a general assembly, but attendance is not compulsory. They also participate in weekly sessions in which they quiz one another to determine whether they have been mastering and integrating the material. These quiz sessions are carried out in small groups with six to ten students and a faculty member or an advanced student.

Cross and other researchers have noted that, despite testimonials by its advocates, little is known about the effectiveness of the auto-tutorial method. The most distressing problem is that we do not know much about the relative merits of the various components of A-TI. Our guess, however, is that the aspect most appreciated by students is the small, integrative quiz session rather than any of the elaborate programmed instructions or tape-directed activities. In short, the anonymity of the lecture class is broken down by the intimacy of the small seminar, not by the packaged self-discovery approach. If we are right, one implication is that when individualized instruction is working effectively, it is not only packaging learning in smaller units but is also creating small-sized learning environments as well. Perhaps the name is a misnomer, since the most important learning, we believe, occurs in the group setting, not in the solitary activity of a student.

A study by Liguori and Harris (1974) revealed data that could be interpreted to support our speculation. They compared the use of personalized systems of instruction with conventional classes and found that there was little difference in performance between the PSI students and the control-group students. The study seemed to contradict all other evidence that PSI-taught students achieved more than those in countless control groups. The distinctive element of the Liguori and Harris study was that the control-group students were attending small lecture classes that approximated the sort of personalized attention that is the hallmark of PSI. Such a finding leads to the conclusion that the crucial factor is not the modularization of learning but rather the interaction between teacher and student or, as is the case with PSI, the interaction between peer tutors and students. We have tacitly assumed that the most important feature of PSI and other individualized instruction programs is their self-pacing methods. Perhaps when these programs succeed in large institutions, it is because they create community and close relationships between teachers and learners rather than because the individualized approach to learning has some special virtue.

In summary, we believe there is a danger in the quick adaptation of individualized instruction to the education of masses of students. Educators may be attributing its success to the wrong characteristics and, in so doing, eliminating those components that improve instruction in massive institutions. The sheer fact that most successful individualized instruction programs incorporate group learning activities signifies that these processes are not, strictly speaking, individualized. Until we know more about individualized instruction, we would argue on behalf of the importance of the nonindividual components. In a provocative essay, Benjamin Green (1974) places considerable emphasis on the role of the surrogate faculty. He writes, "If you can't get undergraduate tutors for love, credit, or money, you ought not to get involved with PSI" (p. 118). Cross (1976, p. 103) adds a final amendment to Green's law when she concludes that PSI is worth trying without peer tutors only if the class is very small. And that, we think, is the point to remember about individualized instruction—not its emphasis on the individual but its success in disaggregating large-scale educational activities into smaller-scale operations.

Consumer Information

In many ways, the consumer movement in higher education is one of the most interesting responses to massiveness in colleges and universities. The need it fills is obvious, but we must be careful; its potential to be used as a defense of big scale is more troublesome. This movement takes its rhetoric from earlier efforts that asserted consumers' rights to know what they were buying as well as the right to challenge the quality of products produced. This concern has surfaced in a new context with two major components: providing educational consumers with honest information about a college, university, trade, or technical school and providing support for students to challenge the institution's performance.

The educational equivalent of truth in advertising is now called an *educational prospectus,* a kind of college catalogue, usually developed by the admissions office in conjunction with the office of institutional research. The major difference between the educational prospectus and a conventional catalogue is that the prospectus does not pretend to paint a glowing picture of life on campus; it is designed to give accurate information to prospective students about what the institution is really like.

In 1975, the Fund for the Improvement of Postsecondary Education launched a National Project and Task Force to consider the concept of better information for student choice. The project brought together eleven institutions that expressed a willingness to develop an educational prospectus. They included a small community college, a business college, a correspondence school, two private residential liberal arts colleges, two rapidly growing urban community colleges, and four large research-oriented public universities—Portland State University, the University of California at Irvine, the University of California at Los Angeles, and the University of Illinois. All of the institutions received assistance from a variety of resource agencies that helped them develop prospectuses. The prospectuses were to include such points as "current regional and national information on the availability of jobs by career field; accurate educational cost projections, descriptions, and explanations of student attrition and retention rates; types of students who are most productive at the institution; current student and faculty perceptions of the quality of the learning processes and student-faculty interactions; the environment of the institution as viewed by various student subcultures; and assessment by graduates of the relationship between their educational experience and job requirements" (Fund for the Improvement of Postsecondary Education, 1976–77, p. 149).

74

Modest Ways to Overcome Massiveness

Each resulting prospectus incorporated important information, often not particularly flattering to the institution. The prospectus for UC Irvine included a survey of reasons students gave for leaving. Prominent among the responses was the impersonality of the campus community (University of California, Irvine, 1976). The university also admitted (p. 34) that since more than 80 percent of its students were commuting, it had a problem trying to overcome the commuters' lack of identity with the campus. At Barat College, a small private liberal arts institution, the prospectus revealed serious weaknesses in the academic program—inadequate library facilities, the existence of departments with only one or two teachers, and the inability to provide enough diversity in course offerings (Barat College, 1976–77). Both institutions balanced this information with reports on other aspects of campus life, such as the excellent research facilities at Irvine and the predominance of small classes at Barat.

We applaud this effort to distinguish what students can reasonably expect from an institution. Furthermore, we note that the schools themselves do not claim this attempt to "tell it like it is" means the institutions intend to sit back and ignore problems, especially those associated with size, just because they have forewarned prospective applicants and enlightened current enrollees. Quite the contrary. The developers of these prospectuses hope that they will serve to inform policy makers about ways in which the institutions can be improved. Institutional information could be developed that exposes the presumed advantages and the disadvantages of scale, as well as reveals weaknesses in the curriculum, counseling and support services, and general administration of the campus. The educational prospectus, then, becomes the first step in a process of self-study and eventual institutional reform.

In the meantime, enrolled students are benefiting from a more realistic picture of what to expect from their college or university. They will know when courses are oversubscribed, what the likelihood is of getting a job with a history major, and what it really takes to complete a degree. These are useful things to know, especially in a massive institution where it is hard to find someone with

75

the information or the time to help students learn how to manipulate the system. Knowledge of this type is power even when students feel powerless to control the policies that make these inconveniences standard operating procedure.

Nonetheless, it is not altogether clear whether applicants will use the information to make wiser choices about where and whether to enroll. Students who have the financial resources to choose among colleges and the grades to gain admission to a variety of programs may find the prospectus helpful in sorting options. But for most students currently interested in pursuing postsecondary education, financial pressures frequently dictate the range of choices —little or no money usually means a student is going to a large public college. As Joan S. Stark (1976, p. 63) observes, "Unless prerequisite questions about financial assistance can be answered, all other disclosures may be largely irrelevant." A survey of high school students conducted by the College Scholarship Service in 1976 substantiated the expectation that the type of institution the student planned to attend was related to family income. "More than three times as many students from high-income families said that they would attend a private institution than did students from low-income backgrounds" ("Making It Count . . . ," 1977, p. 16). In the final analysis, it may not matter what a college chooses to reveal about itself. Students will attend that institution on bases other than rational selection.

The biggest problem with consumer information is that it can justify all kinds of mismanagement merely by describing it. If an institution admits that it is overcrowded, or that it takes on the average five years to complete a bachelor's degree, students will have no cause to complain about being misinformed. In a sense, then, consumer information could serve as an excuse for inaction. An analogy can be made with the labeling of cigarette packs with "Warning: The Surgeon General has determined that smoking is dangerous to your health." The warning absolves the tobacco industry of any responsibility for contributing to cancer. Although information is a first step toward combating massiveness, it is not a sufficient response. The danger is that nothing will change, and students not only will be forced to accommodate themselves to the system as it is, but will also be stripped of the power to express outrage. The institution can respond with a hearty "'I told you so."

The most controversial aspect of consumer education in higher education has been the growing number of suits by students challenging a college or university's failure to provide educational services. The phenomenon is not novel; in western European countries, students are suing institutions for entrance into graduate and professional programs. In West Germany alone, it has been estimated that nearly eight thousand cases are pending charging that universities have failed to provide promised slots at the graduate and professional levels.

Americans have a propensity for litigious activities. So far, the courts have refused to award decisions to students on the basis of academic malfeasance on the part of faculty members or administrators. Students have lost most cases that tried to prove that specific grading policies were unfair or arbitrary. But the courts have taken a more active stance with regard to dismissals for nonacademic reasons.

John H. Mancuso (1976, p. 78) cites the *Dixon* Doctrine (see *Dixon* v. *Alabama State Bd. of Ed.*, 294 F.2d 150 5th Cir. 1961), which "established the precedent that students dismissed from state schools for disciplinary reasons must first have been given at least rudimentary due process protection." Mancuso argues that it is time for the judiciary to broaden its concept of consumer protection, especially in light of the glaring disparity between the bargaining position of a large university and that of the student. Although he does not favor judicial involvement in cases dealing with academic dismissal and grades, he does urge "minimal safeguards" for the truly aggrieved student. Courts, he suggests, should rule on whether students have received a fair hearing before they are dismissed for academic reasons.

Another area where we may see more legal activity concerns contract violations. Students are beginning to charge that institutions are not fulfilling contractual arrangements when classes are canceled or the faculty fails to cover material described in a cat-

77

The Impersonal Campus

alogue. In a recent decision against the University of Bridgeport, the court ruled that the institution failed to provide educational services. Student victories over the higher education system may do more to shake up past practices than the publication of straightforward information. Of course, colleges and universities may retaliate in new and even more bureaucratic ways. For example, general counsels are now combing catalogues to make sure the institution is not promising to deliver anything in writing that can be construed as a contractual arrangement.

One cannot help but notice that, like individualized instruction, consumer information issues emerged as higher education expanded to handle greater numbers of students without proportionately enlarging expenditures or maintaining the crucial features of small-scale operations. Also, it is not surprising that many of the suits are being brought against large institutions. A survey of cases filed in the past five years reveals that 100 percent charged fraud in impersonal educational settings (Fiske, 1977). Small schools may well be guilty of similar practices, but the cases never reach the court stage because they are handled internally. This, too, may say something about a large institution's ability to respond to complaints by individuals. The consumer education movement appears to be more a symptom of the problems associated with bigness than a long-term solution. We would not need to arm ourselves with legal briefs and seek "honest" information if higher education institutions had not taken on the style and impersonality usually found in large profit-making corporations. But, more important, consumer information would not have been as necessary if educators (who seemingly are not in business to make money) paid more attention to the quality of the product and less to devising ways to mass produce it.

Counseling and Support Services

One of the most rapidly expanding areas of higher education, in terms of institutional expenditures and new careers, has been the counseling and student support service function. Over the past two decades, the number of individuals employed by colleges and universities as deans of students, student activity co-ordinators, advisers to student government, counselors, academic advisers, and other noninstructional personnel has grown from less than 40,000 to more than 125,000 (National Center for Educational Statistics, 1971, 1976). Similarly, the share of the institution's budget supporting these kinds of nonclassroom activities has increased significantly. The new professionals are especially visible on the staffs and in the operations of community colleges, large public universities, and institutions that have recently experienced rapid growth. How do we account for this phenomenon? We believe it is at least another attempt to respond to the problems of massiveness, rather than a new concern for student development.

When higher education opened its doors to the masses, it became imperative that institutions find ways to deal with a variety of student needs outside the classroom. The first need was directly related to the financing of their education. Someone had to explain complex financial aid systems to incoming and currently enrolled students, as well as regulate loans, grants, and work-study packages. When registration became too complex and time consuming to be handled by humans alone, someone had to counsel students about the fine points of computer-based scheduling. Housing, social activities, cultural experiences, and the daily business of getting by in a large bureaucracy had to be coordinated and made understandable to freshmen and upper-level students.

In earlier times and in smaller colleges and universities, one all-purpose student affairs dean, with the help of an associate dean and some part-time student interns, managed all these areas. Also, information and counseling were provided by students to one another in dormitories. Upperclassmen and women performed these roles, which were a built-in part of the residential character of the campus. If students desired or needed academic counseling, they usually turned to faculty members. Occasionally, they might attend a bureau of study counsel or specially organized student tutoring program if they were having problems with their studies. A dean of freshmen or dean of studies, who was usually plucked from among the faculty, handled academic problems.

The Impersonal Campus

But with the proliferation of courses, the lack of a general education requirement, and the existence of even more rigidly specified requirements for a major, students now need help determining what to take and when, especially if courses have more students enrolled than they can accommodate. In many institutions, academic advising has become a separate personnel role. Students' major advisers may continue to guide students' studies in a specific area of concentration, but other advising is carried out by persons who often do not hold teaching positions or are in some fashion divorced from the regular faculty and deemed support staff.

The transformation of colleges and universities into larger bureaucracies has all too frequently meant that particular functions related to teaching, learning, and the quality of life on campus have been isolated as separate administrative units. And despite the hard work of persons assigned to these units, the general effect has been to further fragment the sense of community within the institutions and create an uncomfortable academic analogy to the welfare system. When students do not get proper attention or service, or when they need information about a particular area, they run to a person, office, or agency that may know a great deal about a specialized topic but cannot change conditions within other areas of the university. For that matter, specialists seldom feel empowered to alter practices within their own areas of expertise. The best they can do is to ameliorate the student's immediate discomfort by helping to fill out a financial aid form, find lodging, track down a missing recommendation, or locate a faculty member.

Some institutions assign each student a general counselor to whom the student turns for every kind of support service. In the City University of New York, during the open admissions era, it was estimated that one counselor served every 480 students (Staten Island Community College, 1975). In special programs for underprepared students, the figure was closer to fifty to one. Implementing a system of general counseling did not necessarily mean that other student affairs personnel were eliminated. Instead, the common practice involved discussions between general counselors and specific personnel to solve an individual's problems. Students frequently were not party to these discussions. Occasionally, students were told to do the negotiating for themselves, but this was time consuming and took them away from their studies. Counselors then wound up carrying proxies for the students they served and learned the ropes for them.

Measuring the effectiveness of these new support service professionals has been difficult. But judging by retention rates, some counselors succeed in keeping their students in college, and the students themselves testify to the importance of the counseling. They report that their interactions with counselors often represent the only genuine attention they receive on campus (Cohen, 1971). It is hard to imagine how students would survive the onslaught of forms, regulations, and procedures without an advocate or translator of bureaucratic jargon. Without doubt, the services of these counselors are essential to give students somewhere to turn.

However, there are dangers to this response, especially if it is taken to its logical extreme. Looking at the somewhat analogous welfare system, one might make a case that its purpose is to provide service to persons unable to provide for themselves. Very often this entails the considerable involvement of social workers, who help get jobless persons employed or provide assistance to disabled individuals. Critics of welfare maintain that one of its goals should be to empower individuals rather than create even greater dependence on state or federal supports. We would agree. But welfare work begins with the reality that, for a variety of reasons, people ask for help because they are in need of work, food, shelter, and counseling. Their problems are generated not by the welfare system (at least not initially) but by economic and social conditions outside that system.

Similarly, students are becoming increasingly dependent on student affairs personnel, but not because they come to a college or a university with problems. The institutions themselves are generating the problems and creating the dependencies. Students often assume that they are in control until they set foot on campus and realize that they cannot maneuver around the red tape and layers of bureaucracy that characterize massive higher education institu-

81

tions. They start out independent and wind up less autonomous, feeling that they cannot rely on themselves to manage their own lives. Student services personnel become the crutches on which they lean to get through the system. And so, ironically, the counselor may embody some of the problems associated with massiveness. The counselor, not the student, learns how to manipulate the system directly, although some students pride themselves on their ability to manipulate the counselor. In the long run this system only serves to make students more dependent on others.

There is another problem with the dependencies generated through the use of an army of student personnel officers. Welfare makes no pretense about its role as a social service agency. But colleges and universities claim that they exist for an educational purpose. There is something disturbing about the policies and operations of an educational institution that make students less capable of solving their own problems after they arrive than before they came.

These comments should not be interpreted as an attack on student activities personnel. Nor are they intended to undermine the real services they provide. The problem lies in college and university administrators relying too heavily on support services to counteract the negative consequences of massiveness. It may be a logical response but not a long-term solution. And, we fear, supportive services create a troubling atmosphere of students' dependence and passiveness; they give up trying for themselves and begin to count too heavily on the efforts of others. The image of the learner-centered, benevolent counselor, smiling and wise, working to help students overcome difficulties can quickly turn into another, insidious image in which overworked counselors are used by the institution to keep the students quiet, creating the illusion that people care when they really do not. (In some programs for minority students, one gets the uneasy feeling that counselors have allowed themselves to become extensions of a plantationlike mentality where all they have to do is keep the slaves in line.)

Advocating for students within a large institution and simultaneously teaching them to advocate for themselves is a difficult and complex task. Sometimes it seems far easier to do the work for them.

Modest Ways to Overcome Massiveness

But that is frequently educationally unsound and counterproductive to the goals of the institution. As one report comments, "It is ironic that some institutions of higher education [that] have as their mission to teach people to evaluate data, to learn, to test conclusions, to make decisions are themselves so poor at providing students with information and materials vital to the decision making process." ("Making It Count . . . ," 1977, p. 12). The typical institutional response to students appears to be "It's too complicated"; and so experts are hired to perform the job.

Some Modest Proposals

What can be done about massiveness without spending large sums of money or creating new problems? There are three broad areas of fertile soil where improvements could take hold, making campuses more hospitable for human habitation. They are structural organization, residential climate, and teaching and learning modes. What follows is a listing of improvement possibilities within each area. The list is obviously not definitive; in fact, we hope this enumeration will generate other responses that may be more appropriate to particular institutional settings.

Structural Organization. Responses that do not change the content of the curriculum or the teaching styles of the faculty but merely change the scheduling and organization of courses and classes fall under the heading of structural organization. Perhaps the most obvious example of a structural change is the weekend college concept, which has caught on especially in large institutions and among smaller private colleges looking for ways to increase their enrollment. Basically, weekend colleges package courses and curriculums that would ordinarily take place two or three days a week for fifteen weeks, compressing the work into six to eight consecutive weekends of intensive study.

We are not suggesting that all massive institutions redesign their course offerings following the weekend college model, but there are good reasons for considering different ways to provide education, especially if these ways minimize registration hassles, the

83

impersonality of the campus, and the sheer number of people inhabiting overcrowded spaces. For example, colleges and universities that cater to a commuting population might try rescheduling all programs so that students can sign up for one or two days of intensive work. Instead of a weekend college, they would be instituting different weekday colleges. Students would get to know other students in "Tuesday" college well, rather than not knowing anyone throughout the week. The similarity of schedules would establish a sense of community and esprit around a single school day. In one sense, this approach is not unlike taking out subscriptions to the theatre or the symphony. If patrons sit anywhere in the auditorium over the course of a year, they may not ever get the chance to meet other theatre or music lovers. But if they are regular subscribers, assigned the same seat week after week, they invariably strike up conversations with persons sitting next to them. At least the idea of structuring familiarity among students and faculty should be tried in large institutions.

Another structural change related to the all-day college concept is block scheduling. Reports on programs for disadvantaged students suggest that assigning the same thirty freshmen to three courses back to back or throughout the week reduces attrition and strengthens the students' ties to the institution. Many schools are using some variant of block scheduling even when the courses seem totally unrelated. The concept was successfully implemented with Chicanas at San Jose City College, which deliberately scheduled classes for the same group (Guitierrez, 1975).

Unfortunately, some schools have introduced block scheduling as part of a team-teaching project. Team teaching is expensive and time consuming and the educational benefits have not been clearly identified. Block scheduling does not entail significant additional costs and can serve as a useful proxy for the experience of dormitory living, especially if there are places and times between classes in which the same group of learners can discuss a previous class before going into another section. The key element in block scheduling is the familiarity students begin to have with one another

84

on the basis of shared experiences. For older women students returning to higher education, block-scheduled programs have led to the development and implementation of daycare activities and consciousness-raising groups on campus. All students may need is a structure that encourages them to get to know one another.

One interesting variation on the block scheduling idea is being tested at the University of Washington. To combat students' writing problems, the university has designated writing labs that are assigned as adjunct learning units (with credit) to larger discipline-based lecture classes. It is the educational equivalent of the space shuttle. The writing lab rests on the back of the lecture, but it takes the student farther along. In the lab, students work in small groups to prepare written assignments for the larger class. Although the model was designed to ameliorate writing problems, it also is a positive response to massiveness, since it gives the students curricular continuity—what they do in one class integrates with other academic work. Students in the lab build bonds through talking about common writing problems.

Residential Climate. Perhaps the biggest obstacle to creating a sense of community and small scale on a large campus is the absence of opportunities to share living quarters in dormitories or houses. A group living situation provides students with a variety of ways to learn what has not been successfully transmitted in more formal learning settings. A commuting institution is at a distinct disadvantage in terms of its impact on learners while they attend. How can nonresidential institutions, already frequently overcrowded, create some of the conditions of residentiality when students do not live on campus? At the University of California at Irvine, administrators and faculty members have developed residential houses in which commuting students can find fellowship with other students based on a shared interest in a particular subject. The residential houses offer symposiums, meals, lectures, and a place to go whenever a student is on campus. Because students join on the basis of intellectual concerns, such as music or a foreign culture, residence houses appear to be an important alternative to languishing in the

85

The Impersonal Campus

student union or feeling lonely in the commuting students' lounge. The reemerging popularity of sororities and fraternities may also be a response to the impersonality of large schools.

Other efforts to establish a sense of community on a commuting campus involve the establishment of food and student-service cooperatives and student-run hostels, which set aside places where commuters can spend the night or at least have a spot to put their books and clothing. Women's centers and ethnic clubs serve a variety of campus needs. We usually assume that they exist merely as launching pads for confrontations with the administration over sexist or racist policies, but these groups also serve as a rallying point for persons in search of community after they have found the campus lacking. Perhaps this is one reason why women's centers and women's studies courses have taken their greatest hold in large public universities (Howe, 1977).

Unfortunately, colleges and universities are financially strapped, which leaves them few ways to launch community centers and community-building activities. One possible solution to the space problem is to share rooms among different campus groups. Why close certain administrative offices in the daytime or evening when students might have a proper use for them? We believe that more interaction among students, faculty members, and staffers outside the regular avenues of advising, counseling, and management provides a real opportunity for the creation of community. For example, "interconstituency" sports—such as a softball game pitting the French department and its majors against a team of Spanish teachers and students—might be an appropriate way to break down the impersonality of the campus. Joint theatrical productions—outside the drama department—also have a way of giving students a feeling of involvement in campus life. The lesson to be learned is that administrators and faculty members in large institutions must be particularly vigilant to make sure they are providing opportunities for students to participate. Surely we can create ways to engage students in the life of the academy beyond serving them as a captive audience.

Perhaps one reason commuting students fail to get involved

86

in campus life is that faculty and administrators are equally un-involved—they do not hang around after classes either. One possible remedy is to ask a faculty member to commit himself to being on campus and leading a discussion group once a month. In this way, there would be intellectual stimulation for both faculty and students. If staff members were interested, students might be more inclined to take the nonclassroom learning experience seriously. Currently, we hire student activities directors to run our concerts and lecture programs or to organize the intramural sports events. But what if the staff and student volunteers planned and participated in campus-wide activities? Such efforts would be appropriate measures of community service in evaluating faculty promotion.

Food has a way of serving as a focal point for thought and discussion. Recently a bookstore in Washington, D.C., opened a cafe called "Afterworks." Customers can browse through the magazines and books and drink espresso at the same place. At the very least, large campuses might experiment with coffee shops attached to the library or campus bookstore.

Students at large commuting institutions deserve an academic life even if they do not live on campus. Merely attending classes is not a sufficient immersion in the academic world. Extracurricular activities have to be imaginative and include all members of the campus community. It should be possible to make the benefits of residentiality available to those who cannot afford the time or money to spend four years sequestered on a campus.

Teaching and Learning Modes. The availability of small classes throughout a four-year traditional academic program is a logical but costly answer to massiveness. Unfortunately, institutional budgets are based on a funding pattern that offers lower-division students few small classes, while seminars and group discussions are available for upper-division students. We urge a reexamination, perhaps even a reversal, of the funding and resource allocation patterns of large and small classes, especially in massive institutions. During the first two years of college, students would learn in small groups, and then, as they came to understand the institution and their place in it, they would complete their studies in larger settings.

The Impersonal Campus

In some large universities, there are so many majors in certain departments that it might be possible to design a senior majors lecture program, in which students would work independently and attend lectures by different members of the department. Faculty members might even discuss their current research interests, and students would be asked to critique the professor.

Most universities would probably stop short of this suggestion, but one modest idea concerns reorganizing classes to give deliberate attention to community building. Longer classes that meet in students' homes, as well as on campus, should be tried. Group research projects might be a useful antidote to the drone of a lecturer and ought to be implemented along with the technique of splitting up students alphabetically into discussion groups. The faculty might want to review its student assignments to determine whether professors are using class time as efficiently as possible. Are the hours spent in class helping the faculty member get a sense of the students' progress through the semester? Are students addressing one another or only directing their attention to what the teacher wants? A single term paper and a final examination may not be useful teaching and evaluation tools when a faculty member has so few interactions with students outside the classroom. Asking groups of students to develop a particular project might encourage communication outside class and conversation among students and faculty members. An institution in which students are coming and going without an opportunity to linger over a cup of coffee or head for the library after a particularly stimulating class means that those times that are highly structured must be doubly effective.

Summary

We have tried to cast an objective, if wary, eye at current efforts by colleges and universities to offset massive size. The task facing reformers is not easy, particularly in these times of retrenchment and steady-state financing. Nevertheless, we have encountered a genuine concern on the part of faculty members and administrators about what can be done. Everyone seems to agree that massiveness is a problem and that institutions are rapidly losing any claim to being thought of as learning communities. Although there is no one foolproof method of reducing the scale of large institutions (short of razing them and starting all over), we are convinced that more experiments can and should be tried. What is needed is the will power to buck a system. By its very size, the system persuades reformers that all incremental change is not worth struggling for. As a result, some educators have left these massive arenas and are developing colleges on a small scale outside the system. In the next chapter we will look at a number of efforts to establish community-based postsecondary education. The problem facing these educational programs is not how to establish community—it is already there—but rather how to maintain it.

CHAPTER SIX

━━

Alternative Colleges for Atypical Students

━━

The typical undergraduate has been defined as "someone who possesses the most frequently occurring input characteristics and who encounters the most frequently occurring environmental experiences" (Astin, 1971, p. 5). In this sense, the typical full-time freshman is eighteen years old, white, Christian, and male. He attended a public high school, where he attained a grade point average of about B−. He is enrolled in a public coeducational university, lives in a dormitory during his first year, and gets most of his financial support for college from his parents.

Even among such "typical" undergraduates, preferences about institutional size and reactions to scale differ. Some students prefer the anonymity of a big university setting, while others are attracted to more intimate college environments. For example, studies of demographically typical students by Heist and Bilorusky (1970, p. 89) indicate that the clientele of smaller cluster colleges tends to differ from students in larger institutions. "Students in cluster colleges are less vocationally oriented," they note, "particularly with respect to their education, and more predisposed to taking an active role in their education." They profess greater interest in personal development outcomes of education; they are in search of "individual study" and the "development of self-insight." The advantages of smallness—cohesiveness, community, friendliness, and warmth—have special significance for them, even though small is not necessarily beautiful for all students.

But if such differences in educational goals and learning styles lead even "typical" college students to prefer differently sized institutions, what about the reactions to institutional size of more atypical, or nontraditional, students? How does this new clientele fare in smaller colleges? Do they even enroll if given the chance?

Unfortunately we have little evidence to answer these questions, since most nontraditional students attend local and low-tuition institutions—large commuting colleges or state universities, notoriously devoid of cluster colleges or the benefits of residential or community life. Some evidence exists that smallness as an institutional characteristic has had particular historical meaning for one minority group: black students in search of community. Thus, the predominantly black institutions, especially the private liberal arts colleges, traditionally relied on small size and residential education to create a counterculture to combat the destructive elements of racism outside their walls. Students felt a sense of belonging to the institution that mitigated the alienation many experienced when separated from home and family. As Jencks and Riesman (1969, p. 456) suggest, "Residential education has been of the most decisive importance in deprovincializing Negroes from farms, small towns, urban ghettoes, as well as sheltering them from the punishments of the housing market and other forms of local white hostility." It is ironic that smallness, in this instance, was used as a buffer to protect black students from white abuse, but it also had

Alternative Colleges for Atypical Students

the effect of reenforcing racial separation. Small scale and attention to undergraduate teaching have distinguished the predominantly black institution, and most faculty members and administrators on these campuses continue to claim that the key to their success is the attention a small institution can give to its learners (Institute for Services to Education, 1973).

Community-Based Colleges

There is another way to examine how other groups of nontraditional students react to scale. During the past decade, a new kind of postsecondary education institution has emerged that appears to be particularly effective with nontraditional students— adults, low achievers, low-income students, and especially persons from various racial and ethnic backgrounds. These institutions have been labeled "community-based" colleges, "feeder" institutions, "bicultural" learning centers, and "free universities." A prospective student would not find these colleges mentioned in Lovejoy's *Guide to Colleges and Universities,* although many are accredited independently or through association with other colleges and universities. A mere listing of their names reveals their youthfulness and appeal: Colegio Cesar Chavez, Malcolm-King: Harlem College Extension, Oglala Sioux Community College, and Universidad Boricua. Whether the community served is a sparsely populated Indian reservation or an overcrowded, sprawling urban ghetto, these new colleges attempt to build a sense of cohesion and attention to individual learning into their curriculum. Also, these institutions have emerged in response to the realization that there were few alternatives to the "melting pot" ideology of traditional postsecondary educational institutions.

In a sense, the phrase *community-based* reflects a three-pronged concept. First, these colleges believe that educational institutions derive their purpose and programs from identifying and serving the needs of the local geographical community. (In this, their rhetoric is no different from that of the mission of the community college; in practice, however, it means something quite dif-

93

ferent.) Second, these colleges have an obligation to transmit and maintain the values and culture of their immediate community as well as to educate students to survive in the broader society. And finally, the schools insist that students must be educated in ways that affirm individual and group needs through the creation of manageable learning environments. Not surprisingly, then, these institutions have a number of common features, the most obvious of which is size—they are all small. In addition, since many of the community-based colleges are located in urban settings or serve an older, working clientele, they apply creative solutions to the problem of establishing a sense of community within the enterprise without relying on on-campus residences or an elaborate physical plant.

Community-based colleges are filling educational needs that community colleges were designed to serve. In the late 1960s, educational policy makers believed that most minority and older students were being accommodated in community colleges. After all, during the 1960s, two deliberate social policies brought new post-secondary educational opportunities to millions of high school graduates. First, local, state, and federal governments reduced the cost barriers by offering subsidies to students and by building and subsidizing low-tuition community colleges. Second, some educational institutions reduced the barrier of selective admissions by lowering or abandoning requirements for high academic performance in high school and on standardized achievement tests. Many minority and older students did in fact enroll in the new public two-year institutions. But it became increasingly clear that a majority of these new students were, as Cross reported in 1971, young Caucasians who were recent high school graduates.

In the City University of New York (CUNY) in 1969, only 3 percent of the undergraduate population was black and 1 percent was Puerto Rican. Advocates for open admissions argued that an "open door" program would succeed in enrolling more minority students. They projected, for example, that through open admissions programs, in the fall of 1970, 11.7 percent of the total university enrollment would be Puerto Rican. This figure represented the total number of Puerto Rican high school graduates in New York City.

Alternative Colleges for Atypical Students

The achieved enrollment was approximately 4.7 percent, and the vast majority of these students were enrolled in CUNY's community colleges (Office of Institutional Research, 1976). Once in school, these students found that admittance into an open door college did not ensure an education. Retention and attrition rates in CUNY community colleges closely approximated national averages—that is, nearly three quarters of all students enrolling in community colleges did not persist to graduation. We now know that low achievers or low-income students who attended two-year colleges or large institutions were "less likely than were low achievers or low-income students in other institutions to attain the degree" (Holmstrom, 1973, p. 11). Although community colleges may have been designed to provide educational opportunities for new ethnic or nontraditional older students, they had the effect of giving another push to the by now well-known "revolving door." It is difficult to know who is leaving and who is staying, since many institutions do not report an ethnic breakdown of attrition rates, but we can safely assume that minority students are not surviving any better, and perhaps they are leaving in even greater numbers, than their white counterparts. Gittell and Dollar (1974, p. 40) have offered a convincing explanation for the emergence of community-based postsecondary education institutions. "For one thing, minorities have been denied access to established institutions in anything remotely approaching their proportion in the lower school population. Furthermore, minority students who have gained entrance suffer unusually high attrition rates. Dropping out has usually been attributed to cultural alienation experienced by minority students at white institutions and the failure of these institutions to develop programs and facilities directed toward the needs of minority students. Even programs especially designed for minority students frequently have clearly, if not blatantly, assimilationist aims."

Some minority adults, especially workers, may have experienced even greater difficulty enrolling in the already existing community colleges. Open admission, as practiced in New York City, was only available to recent high school graduates. Financing an education, although difficult, was not an insurmountable problem,

95

since most community colleges were low cost or tuition free. However, many older students could not overcome the difficulties of holding down a job or managing a family and being a full- or even part-time student. Family obligations often collided with course scheduling and academic practices even in evening schools. Also, these learners may not have believed that they would be well served by the often cold, impersonal environments that were developed to deliver education to masses of students. In a recent survey, one group of students who had enrolled in a community-based program indicated that they preferred their institution to the local community college because (1) they felt they were receiving more individualized attention; (2) they sensed that they belonged to a learning community; and (3) they believed that the institution incorporated the ideology of cultural pluralism as part of its curriculum. The fact that they could elect black studies courses in an otherwise assimilationist community college did not demonstrate that the institution respected them or their cultural traditions (Malcolm-King: Harlem College Extension, 1975).

Community-based colleges are enrolling a diverse group of nontraditional learners who are not being well served by more traditional institutions. In some community-based institutions, as much as one quarter to one third of the students have tried community colleges and failed or have been failed by them. Another quarter deliberately choose these nonmainstream institutions because they are closer to home. Some go because they believe they can catch up in a less alienating and threatening environment, and finally some are attracted to these institutions because they represent an alternative to the traditional, comprehensive Anglo-conforming community college. Occasionally, community-based programs attract students because they are the only higher education institution available to those who do not wish to or cannot leave home. Location has been an especially important factor in rural communities that have been overlooked by educational planners and assumed not to have a sufficient applicant pool to warrant the establishment of a traditional state-financed institution. One example fitting this last category is community-based education for American Indians.

Alternative Colleges for Atypical Students

Before 1966, only three postsecondary institutions in this country were specifically created to serve the higher education of American Indian students—Haskell Indian Junior College (founded in 1878), Southwestern Indian Polytechnic Institute (founded in 1902), and the Institute for American Indian Arts (established in 1938). If Indians wished to go to college, they had to leave the reservation to attend a non-Indian institution or one of the schools funded and administered through the Department of the Interior's Bureau of Indian Affairs. Generally, these schools offered Indian high school graduates the opportunity to pursue vocational education.

In 1966, the Navajo tribe chartered the first Indian-controlled postsecondary education institution in the country. While the community college offers a number of vocationally oriented programs, it also develops basic skills and offers a general education curriculum designed to ease the transition of Indian students from the reservation into larger state colleges and universities. By 1976, nineteen other tribes were operating such programs and another six were in the process of planning tribally chartered colleges. The establishment of many Indian-controlled institutions followed the passage of Public Law 93-638, "The Indian Self-Determination Act" of 1972, which acknowledged the right of tribes to determine how tribal funds will be administered and which social services will be given highest priority.

In 1970, only 1.5 percent of rural or reservation Indians sixteen years or older had completed college, the lowest proportion of college-educated persons in any American population group (Locke, 1976). A few existing colleges and universities were willing to develop extension centers on the reservation. The Indian satellite campuses form one model. They were established by Northeast Nebraska Technical Community College on the Winnebago, Santee Sioux, and Omaha reservations and administered by an all-Indian board of regents deriving its authority from the board of governors of the community college. A more common model is based on a tribally chartered institution that contracts with a state college merely for the transfer of credit and awarding of degrees.

The largest Indian-controlled college, Navajo Community

97

College, has a total enrollment of 300 full-time students; the smallest, Standing Rock Community College, has less than fifty. One might argue that Indian postsecondary education institutions are small because of their rural isolation and their tiny potential applicant pool, in comparison with other state institutions. But these are only partial explanations. The sense of community runs deep within each tribe and within each clan belonging to the tribe. To the outside observer, the existence of three separate colleges to serve the learning needs of Indians on adjacent reservations appears unjustified. But if one considers the exceedingly high dropout rate of Indian students who leave their homes to attend institutions beyond the reservation, the concept of small, community-oriented learning units makes some sense. On the Pine Ridge reservation alone, with thirty-five thousand people living on a land base the size of Rhode Island, there are nine different towns or communities, each twenty to thirty miles apart. Oglala Sioux Community College has established learning centers in each of these communities. Although the total size of the college may be 250 students, these students are being educated in learning environments of perhaps twenty-five students each. Limited transportation, as well as the importance placed on learning within one's own community, dictates both the function and form of much Indian-controlled postsecondary education. In this sector, small is not only beautiful, it is essential for institutional effectiveness.

Interestingly, the conditions that gave rise to community-based Indian postsecondary education differ markedly from the conditions under which community-based urban colleges arose. Malcolm-King: Harlem College Extension and Universidad Boricua did not have a limited applicant pool from which to select students. Furthermore, they were not constrained by geography, inadequate transportation, or the existence of already established living communities isolated from one another. Both colleges emerged as planned educational alternatives for black and Spanish-speaking populations in New York City. Nevertheless, their founders made the deliberate choice to keep both institutions small—Malcolm-King has decided on a limit of 800 students; Boricua's optimum student population is 300. This choice of size was based on the fact that existing institutions in the metropolitan area were either providing inadequate service to their students or, worse yet, giving no service at all.

In 1968, there was no college exclusively designed to meet the educational needs of the adults living in Harlem. Recent high school graduates, if they met entrance criteria, could enroll in one of the branch campuses of CUNY. True, those younger students who did enter CUNY often dropped out, but the problem of the older students was even greater—they had difficulty even enrolling. In the spring of 1968, a group of Harlem civic leaders persuaded Marymount Manhattan College to offer a pilot course in basic skills at the local elementary school. Eventually two other institutions, the College of Mount St. Vincent and Fordham University (both in the Bronx), joined Marymount to sponsor Malcolm-King. Faculty members recruited from the three institutions teach as volunteers in classrooms and offices provided free to the college by local community school boards and agencies (most of the college's courses were held in the classrooms of a local public school). By the fall of 1976, Malcolm-King had enrolled 700 students.

Up until 1973, there was no Puerto Rican college in America, not even in New York City, where nearly 60 percent of the Puerto Rican population in the mainland United States lives. Puerto Rican students wishing to pursue postsecondary education in New York City had few options. Even the creation of the bilingual Hostos Community College in the South Bronx in 1970 left many older Puerto Rican students in other boroughs of the city without an opportunity to pursue college-level work on an individualized, part-time basis. In 1973, Universidad Boricua was established in the Williamsburg section of Brooklyn to serve working Puerto Rican students. It now enrolls more than 200 students. Unlike Malcolm-King and many Indian-controlled community colleges, Boricua is *free standing;* that is, the college does not have any formal structural affiliation for the awarding of credits or degrees with another college or university.

Both Malcolm-King and Universidad Boricua wanted to reverse students' feelings of failure with academic work, as well as

99

counteract a sense of alienation from education. They implemented educational programs that emphasized counseling and planned faculty-student interaction. Students would not face a large impersonal environment. The first evidence prospective applicants had that they were being treated differently from their peers in CUNY was the insistence at both institutions on personal interviews as part of the admissions procedure. Those who have attended small, highly selective colleges are familiar with personal interviews, but these are rarely if ever experienced by newcomers to a large public institution. Although the programs were nonselective, that is, they stated that they would accept all high school graduates and even some students without a diploma, this procedure gave applicants the impression that Malcolm-King cared about them and their application to their studies. Although Malcolm-King offers only the first two years of a college program, it nevertheless is eager to distinguish itself from the large, publicly supported two-year community colleges. Because of its private sponsorship by three four-year institutions and the fact that a Malcolm-King degree is automatically accepted by those institutions, Malcolm-King could be viewed as a cluster college, offering a general education, even though it also awards two-year terminal degrees in early childhood education and business.

In addition to the personal interview, Malcolm-King has developed a number of structures that, taken together, reinforce the concept of community. Unlike the comprehensive community college, Malcolm-King focuses on academic programs and career tracks that relate to practical community needs. They are not trying to offer all things to all people. For example, the college's early childhood education program grew out of the needs of the Central Harlem Association of Montessori Parents and carries a prescribed core curriculum, which every student must take. All Malcolm-King students are required to enroll in a special course entitled "Introduction to College Study and Research Skills" if they cannot demonstrate writing proficiency on entrance. The course encompasses both cognitive and affective learning objectives and is taught jointly by faculty members and counselors. Students do not even receive credit for this class until they pass the proficiency exam.

Alternative Colleges for Atypical Students

Clearly, the freshman year at Malcolm-King differs markedly in structure and philosophy from that in many educational institutions serving older black adults. A considerable amount of core work is required of all students, and since the load is so demanding, students must petition to take more than six credits per semester. Courses meet one or two nights a week and generally run two to three hours. Administrators at Malcolm-King argue that because a course may only meet once a week, it is imperative that students attend regularly. Attendance is required for all classes, and students are warned that they may only have two absences per semester. This apparently regimented approach gives students a sense that they belong to a small, serious learning community, as well as a sense that they will be held accountable for their actions.

Universidad Boricua takes a different approach to the uses of smallness to create community. Each student designs a program for study by writing a learning contract composed of a list of objectives and an outline of the experiences to accomplish them. The Universidad is thus conceived as a learning resource at the service of the student. Once students have developed the contract, they engage in the learning process through contact with facilitators using the Puerto Rican community as their classroom. As Gittell and Dollar (1974, p. 44) have observed, "Classes are held wherever students and facilitators decide to meet: somebody's house, a local library, walking through the streets, or in Boricua's learning center. . . . Universidad Boricua is part of the community. So often facilitators identify individuals in the community who have their own knowledge of how the community runs—not because they have a degree, but because they have lived there—and ask them to come in and share their knowledge." At Universidad Boricua there is no distinction between town and gown. The living community is an integral part of the learning community. The benefits of residence on campus are created by building an educational program on community ties and resources.

The Chicano subculture is also being served by community-based institutions. In the past five years, more than half a dozen new Chicano colleges have been established in the Southwest and

101

Far West. They include D-Q University, Colegio de la Tierra, and Universidad de Camposines Libres in California; Universidad Jacinto Trevino, Hispanic International University, and Juarez-Lincoln University in Texas; and Colegio Cesar Chavez in Oregon. Together they enroll approximately two thousand students. Although each college has a distinctive approach to bilingual, bicultural education, they all share a common characteristic—smallness.

Colegio Cesar Chavez has developed a special integration of the concept of community within its educational ideology. The Colegio, the only four-year accredited college in the country operated by Chicanos, began in 1973 when faculty members and students from the Chicano Studies program at Mt. Angel College in Oregon obtained permission to attempt to keep Mt. Angel alive after the church-related institution lost its accreditation (Wuest, 1976). These Chicano educators developed a community-based, *familia*-oriented education, which stresses the absence of domination of one person by another in the educational process. The Colegio emphasizes the need for individualized education to be guided by the sharing and development of the self with others.

Family cohesion and role status are traditionally important in Mexican-American culture. The notion of family has broader implications in Chicano culture than it does for the majority culture. It transcends the concept of the extended family to include another value, identified by Ramirez and Castaneda (1974, p. 126) as the "personalization of interpersonal relationships," which the Colegio refers to as the concept of *familia*. Students at Colegio Cesar Chavez become members of a learning-counseling team that includes a core faculty member, at least two adjunct teachers, and a student peer. This team approximates an individual family group and lessens the degree of culture shock that these Chicano students are particularly susceptible to when entering large bureaucratic and alienating institutions. The team provides a supportive milieu and acts as a surrogate family. In addition, each student serves as a peer member on another student's team. Students participate in monthly evaluation meetings with their familia teams in which progress is evaluated and learning objectives are reviewed.

Alternative Colleges for Atypical Students

Colegio Cesar Chavez believes that the familia provides individualized learning for its 100 Chicano students. Previous efforts to introduce learning contracts and individualized courses of study have not met with particular success among Chicanos. Because of their long history of passive learning in the traditional educational system, many students at the Colegio have difficulty asserting themselves. Many of them are unable to identify their educational interests and career goals. In fact, educational programs centered on the individual have tended to isolate the student from other students. The lack of peer support and competition undermined students' motivation to learn. The familia is an attempt to wed self-motivated learning to community. Colegio Cesar Chavez is organized deliberately as a communal environment, and all students participate in the familia, regardless of whether they live on campus. Hence, educators at the Colegio have found another way to offer the benefits of residentiality to nonresident learners by building community into the classroom and curriculum.

The existence of these community-based colleges, no matter how tenuous their funding, indicates that these institutions are filling an educational need not met for many students even though they may have access to large, stable, and richly subsidized two-year and four-year colleges. That students have turned their backs on once-tuition-free CUNY to attend Universidad Boricua, where tuition is $3,000 a year, testifies to the special contribution community-based colleges seem to make. The creation of a community seems to be the key element in their effectiveness, and small size, although not an absolute necessity for producing that element, certainly makes it more possible.

As valuable as Malcolm-King and Colegio Cesar Chavez may be, they face an uncertain future. It is unclear whether these and other community-based institutions can survive another year operating on grants from private foundations and the federal government. Even with outside support, they exist on remarkably meager budgets. Nonetheless, they must deflect a portion of their current monetary and human resources to the tasks of proposal writing, fund raising, and collecting data that can be used to justify

103

their existence to past and future donors and patrons. In addition, the institutions are in a constant struggle to acquire formal legitimacy, which would make them eligible for other types of state and federal funding. They travel a lonely and frequently frustrating course.

The course is lonely in part because most community-based institutions have assumed that to maintain their cohesiveness within, they must minimize ties outside the institution. Although some have arrangements with one or two other colleges, they do not exist as formal units within a broader system, at least not within the higher education systems as they are usually structured. They cannot even find their place among the current crop of associations representing higher education to the public. Recognizing the need for reinforcement from others with similar missions, they have begun to create their own networks. Within the past few years, two new associations have been founded to represent the interests of community-based institutions, as well as to serve their common needs.

The Clearinghouse for Community Based Free Standing Educational Institutions (CBFSEI) is a national membership organization of institutions that are community-controlled and independent of state support. Incorporated in 1976 in Washington, D.C., it operates through membership dues and a grant from the Fund for the Improvement of Postsecondary Education. It boasts thirty members, such as accredited colleges, free universities, and counseling and advocacy centers. The clearinghouse serves as a central coordinating agency for resource sharing and development, information dissemination, technical assistance, and evaluation and impact research on community-based educational programs. One primary activity of the clearinghouse is to advocate CBFSEIs to government and nongovernmental policy makers. It analyzes educational legislation and regulations to determine whether member institutions may participate or whether they are being discriminated against.

The American Indian Higher Education Consortium is another new network whose functions and purposes closely parallel those of the clearinghouse. The consortium, established in 1974 in Denver, Colorado, represents thirteen *mature* tribally controlled In-

104

dian postsecondary education institutions. The consortium has defined *mature* as those colleges that have been officially chartered by
the tribe and are currently serving students. An additional six to
eight Indian-controlled colleges are awaiting tribal approval and
expect to enroll their first class of students in the fall of 1978
(Locke, 1976). Its primary goal is to help establish alternative criteria for the awarding of accreditation. Presently, Indian-controlled
institutions rely on formal and informal arrangements with state
subsidized colleges, such as the affiliation of Oglala Sioux Community College with Black Hills State College in South Dakota. Oglala
Sioux Community College is not currently eligible for direct funding
by federal agencies, except the Bureau of Indian Affairs. It receives
financial support through Black Hills State College, which is
awarded funds to disperse to the Indian-controlled school. Leaders
in the Indian education community believe that the consortium will
generate new methods of assessing the quality of Indian education
that will eventually be adopted by regional accrediting associations.

These networks, along with informal activities jointly sponsored by community-based colleges, seem to have provided some
support for the movement, but if funding the individual small colleges seems tenuous, it is almost impossible to imagine how the clear-
inghouses and the consortiums will survive. Perhaps, in the long run,
they were not meant to survive but merely to promote these new
institutions so that they may acquire new advocates. The predica-
ment may be that to acquire new sources of support, community-
based colleges will have to begin to look and act more and more
like mainstream institutions, thus putting their special missions in
jeopardy.

The small, community-based postsecondary institutions represent such a small fraction of the total higher education enrollment
that some observers say it is not worth paying much attention to
their survival, let alone providing for the emergence of scores of
other new colleges. They say that the problem of educating minority
students must be solved in the larger, more stable, state-supported
university or the locally financed community college. But evidence
continues to mount suggesting that students from a variety of sub-

105

cultures do not fare well in the institutions we have built to hold them. Furthermore, these large institutions systematically socialize such students to reject their own culture and community. The few minority students who persist to graduation are frequently forced to survive by ridding themselves of their heritage and "cultural baggage." A number of educators working within the traditional system despair of any solution. Gilbert D. Roman (Casso and Roman, 1976, p. 170), speaking to a conference on access to higher education for Mexican-Americans, concluded that "no effort within the system is likely to succeed." Roman suggests that Anglo colleges with a high concentration of Chicanos begin establishing links with Chicano alternative education programs. However, one thing is clear—the small, community-based institution offers an important alternative to the mass education of minority students.

CHAPTER SEVEN

Agenda for Action

The size of a college or university affects the nature of its impact on students. Twenty years ago, when fewer students pursued a higher education, they paradoxically had a greater range of learning settings and institutional types from which to choose. Diversity in higher education existed not by design but rather because no central authority was formulating a set of policies that applied to the entire higher education enterprise. The major changes that have occurred in American higher education have been in response to policy decisions made at the federal, state, and institutional levels. These policies provided for the expansion of the public sector, gave limited financial assistance for the economically disadvantaged, and encouraged the education and training of professionals in fields deemed important to the national interest (Astin, 1977, p. 243). The cumulative effect of these policies on the size of institutions has been significant and troubling because it has put a premium on fostering

107

rapid growth. This has radically altered the nature of campus life, student involvement with the faculty, and ultimately the teaching and learning process itself. Until a few years ago, the most telling and graphic example of the lasting legacy of these policies was the slow, yet relentless, reduction in the number of small institutions and, conversely, the seemingly uncontrolled expansion of public institutions and institutional systems.

Recently, this apparently uncontrollable process has begun to lose momentum as the era of rapid growth has been gradually replaced by a period of relatively stable enrollments. Except in a few settings where population shifts and economic conditions continue to create the demand for even more spaces in higher education institutions, the need to provide for increasing enrollments by students of the traditional age has apparently slackened. Thus we are now left with the problem of determining how to best utilize the existing facilities—those massive institutions that have emerged in the past two decades and the smaller ones that have survived this period of rapid growth with their size intact. The question this chapter addresses is, What can educators do now to make the most of bigger schools, or, to paraphrase Clark Kerr, how can we make the university smaller even after it has grown larger? (Kerr, 1968, p. 316).

Change and Financial Constraint

A few years ago, the president of a well-known experimental college concluded that his institution, which had been founded in the late 1960s, would never have gotten off the ground five years later. He argued that after 1970 there was virtually no risk capital available to start new ventures. Perhaps he was correct, since it is logical to assume that the chances for making improvements seemed better in the era of expansion when there was an unlimited sense of confidence in, and support for, higher education. More than a decade ago, money was available to try out such things as cluster colleges and lower student-faculty ratios, but as belt tightening reached even the most financially secure college, there were fewer opportunities to experiment, less money available to make change happen. Some administrators believe the times now demand that they exercise caution and display a talent for maintaining existing programs, especially in light of threatened budget cutbacks and hostile state legislatures. Their concern for preserving the status quo is legitimate but, in our judgment, short-sighted. It might be an effective rear-guard action, preventing further budget losses, but it does not address the need to improve a massive institution's educational effectiveness.

Furthermore, since the massive university is a relatively new educational phenomenon, it seems unwise to talk about maintenance in the absence of knowledge about the kind of education that institution provides. What is it that should be protected from attack? Frequently one of the first items to be eliminated in a budget cut is money for noninstructional student personnel services. Administrators hope to effect savings by reducing these services, which often exist to ameliorate the negative aspects of massiveness. The larger the institution, the greater the need for these services (Packwood, 1977). Yet in an effort to maintain the appearance of academic quality, these supposedly nonessential functions are the first to go. Thus the fundamental error "maintainers" make is assuming that they know how their institution educates students. As a matter of fact, we have precious little information about both the costs and the educational benefits of massive universities.

An equally serious problem arising from the concept of maintaining the status quo in this era of stable enrollment, inflation, and increasing public scrutiny of higher education is that despite the best intentions of conscientious administrators, adjustments are being made anyway. Even if enrollments are not decreasing, inflation is causing colleges and universities to make changes in the ways they deliver services. Maintaining is not what people do in times of economic pressure. Rather, they make adaptations after they have decided what is essential and what can be eliminated. They attempt to find better ways of operating, conserving that which must remain and discarding unessential activities. To a large extent, organizations operate under the same principle—workers may be laid off, plants closed, products altered. The maintainers are fooling themselves if they assume they can forestall change and avoid making the hard decisions. The issue is not whether adjustments will come but whether we can plan those adjustments so that they will not exacerbate the negative consequences of massive higher education.

Economic pressures force change. In most instances, the tendency is to let budgetary actions dictate change rather than to make changes first. While external policies may have produced bigger institutions, internal decision making is now in a position to improve the quality of education that very large schools provide. In fact, the need to examine the resource allocations of an institution may have a salutary effect on academic programming. Thus in one sense the times could not be better for taking a long, hard look at the consequences of twenty years of rapid growth. At long last, educators may be in a position to think about the kinds of trade-offs that were explicitly or implicitly made as they pursued an ideology of bigger is better. If the university was led down this garden path by a variety of suitors, it is not too late to assert control over its own destiny.

Bigger can be better than it currently is. But left unimproved, or, worse yet, left victimized by uninformed choices about the kinds of adjustments they can make, massive institutions will become increasingly less effective educational communities. As a first step toward determining what should be done, administrators could ask themselves and other members of the college community a series of questions such as these:

- Can students name and identify seventy-five other students?
- Can faculty members name and identify twenty-five faculty members in other departments?
- Does it take longer than one hour to fill out registration forms and get them approved?
- Do administrators have time to teach or to serve as academic advisers?
- Does it take a year for a faculty member to get a new course approved on an experimental basis?

110

Agenda for Action

Administrators in small schools might be surprised at the results, since smallness does not automatically guarantee the creation of a learning community. Nevertheless, it is likely that persons in institutions with more than ten thousand students would have greater difficulty responding positively to these questions.

Suppose an institution has grown so large that its constituents are unable to give one positive answer to these questions. What does this represent? In our judgment, the school might be effective at credentialing students, but it is in danger of losing its identity as a learning community. Many behavioral scientists are now suggesting that what students learn in college is a product of what they learn from each other. Both Nevitt Sanford and Theodore Newcomb have emphasized that "what students learn is determined in large measure by their fellow students, or more precisely, by the norms of behavior, attitudes, and values that prevail in the peer groups to which they belong" (Sanford, 1967, p. 175). Unfortunately, much of their work was done in small institutions. In the absence of definite research findings, administrators in larger schools must become their own investigators and weed out those factors that hinder learning from those which enhance it. As we have suggested, it is possible to reduce the *effective* size of an institution without reducing its absolute enrollment by creating or encouraging what are in effect smaller communities within the larger organization. For example, Alexander Astin has suggested that deemphasizing the residential experience in larger institutions has diminished their impact on students. He urges administrators to calculate the costs and benefits of dormitories as measured by degree completion and the implementation of career plans (Astin, 1977, p. 249). This is a task which an office of institutional research and an administrator can easily undertake. In this connection, another interesting concept to explore is the relationship of sororities and fraternities to learning in massive institutions. Our guess is that these nonacademic structures have played a considerable role in creating learning communities on larger campuses. Equally important is a freshman house system during that critical first year so that students are socialized into the

111

world of academe. All of these thoughts are hypotheses that must be tested in *real* situations. Administrators eager to improve the quality of undergraduate education are in an excellent position to compile and analyze the data and make policy decisions in light of the results. This approach to change might be appropriately termed *action/research.*

The Administrator as Activist/Researcher

In the traditional mode of research and development in higher education, research drives action. That is, researchers carry out controlled experiments and create theoretical models of how a program or institution should perform. This format offers the researcher the chance to control the variables and watch the results. On the basis of these experiments, consultants and planners develop model programs that supposedly combine the best features of each experiment. The job of the administrator is relatively easy— adapt this pretested program to the institution. This process could be likened to buying a sewing pattern in a fabric store and then making a garment. The product never quite looks as good as the picture, since the pattern was designed to fit someone else (with perfect proportions). Applying the analogy somewhat differently, we might say that institutions actually should not be buying more models or patterns at this point, because their task is actually to make their ill-fitting wardrobe fit better. A store-bought pattern will not help, since what is needed is an eye for working with the existing materials, reworking the design, trimming here and letting the hem out there.

"Action/research" uses the materials already available and manipulates them until something better is fashioned. It cannot promise to provide the all-purpose pattern, but it may help an institution take full advantage of what that institution has to offer. The premise here is the reverse of that in the traditional approach. The *actions* of the past twenty years must now be *researched.* Thus action drives research rather than the other way around. This means of improving the educational product in massive institutions

112

can be broken down into two dimensions: Action/research concerning the academic program and action/research concerning institutional structures.

The Academic Program. The following is a series of researchable questions that will help administrators understand the relationship of the institution's size to its educational offerings.

1. Has the institution's growth affected the range of courses undergraduates traditionally take in their freshman, sophomore, and junior years? Which students, if any, are taking advantage of the diversity of course offerings?
2. How often do students have the opportunity to write essays during their undergraduate years? How does this figure compare with that in other schools of comparable size?
3. What percentage of an undergraduate's course of study is taken in the discussion/seminar mode? To what extent are freshmen and sophomores exposed to classes in which they can participate as active discussants?
4. What are the common characteristics of successful students in your institution? Are certain departments producing a higher proportion of academic achievers than others? Is there a correlation between the amount of time they spend on campus and their academic success?
5. What reason does the dropout give for leaving? What characteristics do dropouts have in common?

After getting answers to these questions, administrators can make informed choices about the kind of undergraduate education they wish to provide and develop alternative learning programs. For example, if few students are taking advantage of a range of courses in the freshman year, perhaps more classes could be scheduled together and thus afford students the chance to get to know one another within the classroom setting. This would also give faculty members a chance to work as a team comparing students' progress across a number of disciplines. A simple reshuffling of room assignments and class times might go a long way toward creating

113

a sense of community among students and teachers, especially in two-year colleges, where there are so few structures that reinforce the institution's mission as an educational enterprise.

If one of the functions of a liberal education consists of improving a student's writing ability during the college years, then massive institutions must look carefully at the academic program to make sure that students receive enough practice and instruction in writing. If research indicates that they are being asked to write only when they reach their junior and senior years, the institution has diminished by half its ability to have an impact in this area. Furthermore, it has failed to prepare students to take advantage of advanced courses that require even greater facility in the use of the written word. If transcripts of freshmen and sophomores reveal that numbers of students are taking similar courses, writing instruction might be integrated with the content of these courses by having similar themes for the semester graded by peer tutors and upperclassmen. Administrators must weigh the educational losses that may result from allowing students to ignore writing during the first two years of their academic program.

Perhaps the most important and difficult issue to be studied is the comparative costs of different academic programs. We have yet to develop formulas for assessing the costs and benefits of educating students in different institutional settings. At what stage do the limitations of large size so affect a campus learning community that its benefits become negligible and hence its higher cost, as compared with off campus education, ceases to be justified? Is it possible that an Open University system which makes no pretense of creating a campus environment and teaches students in their own homes or work sites via television is just as effective an educational program as that provided by many large state universities that are spending two and three times as much money per student? We must face this question squarely if we expect to receive continued public support for higher education. The list of researchable questions concerning the effectiveness of academic programs in massive institutions is endless and suggests that we will never comprehend the relationship of institutional size to educational quality until we venture beyond comparing seemingly similar variables—the number of courses, credits, hours—to understanding their differential impact.

Institutional Structures. It is always difficult to draw any kind of causal relationship between an institution's structure and its educational effectiveness. But one obvious aspect of the connection between them is whether or not the services staff and the administration reduce the amount of time faculty members and students spend on nonacademic issues. Institutional structures should free individuals to devote their energies to teaching and learning both within and outside the classroom. We hypothesize that massive schools have a tendency to demand more, not less, attention to their operation than do smaller ones, despite the research findings of Baldridge and others (1973). If one examines these findings carefully, one discovers that large institutions often delegate power over certain decisions to departments and faculty members. Thus individuals, especially tenured professors, are left alone to pursue their research unencumbered by having to deal with institutional issues. The focus of decision making has become the comfort of a few members of a department, and in turn these departments exist comfortably as semi-autonomous fiefdoms controlling one arena of university decision making but unable to influence or comment on the decisions of other equally autonomous units. This system, Baldridge claims, demonstrates a surprising lack of bureaucracy. But in fact, it is merely academic anarchy.

The kind of action/research needed to understand how decisions are made in large institutions must begin with an analytical approach to the institution's bureaucracy. Are there situations in which it is essential for academic representatives from more than one department to work together on policy? How many levels of decision making must be passed through for faculty members to introduce a new course or for students to drop a program? What is the procedure for appealing the decisions of a higher authority? These questions begin to flesh out the kind of institutional structures which either reinforce the academic function of the university or undermine it.

The Impersonal Campus

Another important area of institutional governance relates to the proliferation of university-wide regulations when informal agreements would suffice. Our experience might lead us to believe that regulations make the operation of a campus more efficient. However, that is not always the case. It is important to understand which types of regulation have grown over the past decade and how the issues they govern were handled in the past. Perhaps the creation of uniform codes of interaction has not had as salutary an effect on university organization as was once imagined.

What kinds of actions follow from research on these questions of management? The undergraduate enrollment of a big institution might be subdivided administratively and the faculty and staff assigned to work with manageable cohorts of students. As an alternative to centralized personnel offices, it might be preferable to assign counselors to clusters of departments, or financial aid officers to groups of students. In this way, commuting institutions and schools with limited residential facilities could place the support staff in closer contact with its clients.

Simple structural alterations in the delivery of supportive services might also help to reduce the negative aspects of massive institutions. For example, registration procedures could include a mechanism whereby all students would be guaranteed at least one course that is their first choice. If the school did not deliver, the student would receive a tuition reimbursement and get a class for free. Another recommendation is to have counselors see students in groups as well as individually. Frequently those students who need counseling the most do not show up for the personal sessions but may participate in less threatening group experiences. To promote a sense of community, administrators might decide to limit the number of course choices in the freshman year so that students are likely to see familiar faces in their classes.

Given the success of such programs as the weekend college, administrators on campuses that enroll considerable numbers of working and part-time students might well attempt to reorganize their services to make them more coherent. Frequently students who can ill afford to take classes three or four evenings a week might prefer to have all their course work blocked into one or two evenings for five hours each. Faculty members might even prefer such an arrangement because it leaves them longer blocks of time in which to conduct their research. Rescheduling a massive institution to operate according to an "intensive" day or evening program might also make better use of the physical plant by conserving energy. Only those buildings and classrooms that would be needed would be available. Administrative offices could also be utilized more effectively. Finally, students would not waste time and energy commuting back and forth to campus. They would know that they had to be motivated to learn one day a week and would schedule their other responsibilities accordingly.

It is clear, then, that institutional structures help create a climate for learning. As Burton Clark and Martin Trow (1968, p. 122) have written, "It is worth reemphasizing that the organization of a college as a community has profound effects on student life in ways that have been given too little consideration by administrators and too little study by scholars." If the organization of a campus seems designed solely to accommodate the needs of administrators and a select group of the faculty, students will quickly get the message that the environment is dedicated less to learning than it is to management. Students will begin to respect the academic purposes of an institution when they see those purposes reflected in its formal organization. Education cannot take place unless there has been created a small enough community to provide for continuing interpersonal relations. Perhaps training can be conducted in an atmosphere in which community is not necessary, since the goal is merely to master a set of materials. In this instance, an individualized curriculum might be the most appropriate method of delivering services. But if the purpose of the institution goes beyond training to education, it cannot ignore the human dimension. Thus administrators might wish to explore new ways to use space on their campuses, placing administrative offices throughout the community rather than keeping them isolated from the teaching and learning environment. In addition, student space should not be ghettoized in such a way as to keep it removed from

117

the activities of the faculty and noninstructional staff. The continued segregation of functions only exacerbates the undergraduate student's already fragmented perception of the institution's mission.

Summary: Mind over Matter

While the university has many purposes, the education of undergraduate students stands as one of its most important societal responsibilities. Yet over the past two decades, this responsibility has received little attention and even less analysis from campus decision makers and faculties. The guardians of academe merely assumed that the purpose would be served by opening the flood gates and providing a registration card (if not a seat in a classroom) for nearly every student who wished to enroll. But providing access to education is not sufficient. In the rush to open up higher education to the masses, we may have underestimated the ways in which large scale diluted the institution's capacity to serve as a learning community. And, ironically, we may also have undermined the student's motivation to learn by making higher education appear to be so accessible. We offered the illusion of a college education but not its substance.

The real problems facing today's administrator and faculty member are not generated by the threat of external influences over the teaching and learning process. Instead, the difficulties arise because internal control of and influence over that process is lacking. Although there is no perfect size or magic critical mass by which all institutions should be judged, educators must discover that balance between size and function which is essential for effective performance. The appropriate size of a college or university is a function of its purpose. Unless we begin to examine this crucial scale/purpose relationship, especially with regard to the education of undergraduate students, the very large American university, like the dinosaur, may become extinct because "its body became too large for its brain" as Clark Kerr once jokingly remarked. Isn't it time for the university to assert mind over matter?

118

References

ALEXANDER, J. *Report on the Freshman Cluster Program at UMBC.* Unpublished paper submitted to the Fund for the Improvement of Postsecondary Education, Washington, D.C., 1976.

ALFRED, R. "Impacts of the Community and Junior College on Students." Iowa City, Iowa: American College Testing Program, 1975.

ASTIN, A. W., and LEE, C. *The Invisible Colleges: A Profile of Small, Private Colleges with Limited Resources.* New York: McGraw-Hill, 1972.

119

References

ASTIN, A. W. *Predicting Academic Performance in College.* New York: Free Press, 1971.

ASTIN, A. W. *The Myth of Equal Access in Public Higher Education.* Atlanta, Ga.: Southern Education Foundation, 1975.

ASTIN, A. W. *Four Critical Years: Effects of College on Beliefs, Attitudes, and Knowledge.* San Francisco: Jossey-Bass, 1977.

BALDRIDGE, J. V., and others. "The Impact of Institutional Size and Complexity on Faculty Autonomy." *Journal of Higher Education,* 1973, *44* (7), 564–560.

Barat College. "A Prospectus." Lake Forest, Ill.: Barat College, 1976–77.

BARKER, R. G., and GUMP, P. V. *Big School, Small School.* Stanford, Calif.: Stanford University Press, 1964.

BAYER, A. E. "Faculty Composition, Institutional Structure, and Students' College Environment." *Journal of Higher Education,* Sept.–Oct. 1975, pp. 549–565.

BERNSTEIN, A. R. "How Big Is Too Big?" In D. W. Vermilye (Ed.), *Individualizing the System: Current Issues in Higher Education 1976.* San Francisco: Jossey-Bass, 1976.

BLACKBURN, R., and others. *Changing Practices in Undergraduate Education.* Berkeley, Calif.: Carnegie Council on Policy Studies in Higher Education, 1976.

BOWEN, F. M., and LEE, E. C. *The Multicampus University.* New York: McGraw-Hill, 1971.

BOWEN, H. R. *Investment in Learning: The Individual and Social Value of American Higher Education.* San Francisco: Jossey-Bass, 1977.

BOWERS, W. J. "Student Dishonesty and Its Control in College." New York: Bureau of Applied Social Research, Columbia University, 1964.

BOYLE, B. M. "University Giantism: Beneficial or Detrimental?" Unpublished paper. Greensboro: University of North Carolina, 1976.

BRENEMAN, D. "Report on Interinstitutional Cooperation." Canton, N.Y.: College Center of the Finger Lakes, 1976.

BURN, N. *Report on the Five Colleges, Inc., Project.* Unpublished

References

report submitted to the Fund for the Improvement of Postsecondary Education, Washington, D.C., 1976.

BUSHNELL, R. A., and ELGIN, D. S. "The Limits to Complexity: Are Bureaucracies Becoming Unmanageable?" *The Futurist,* Dec. 1977, pp. 337–351.

Carnegie Commission on Higher Education. *New Students and New Places.* New York: McGraw-Hill, 1971.

Carnegie Commission on Higher Education. *The More Effective Use of Resources.* New York: McGraw-Hill, 1972.

CARTTER, A. M. *An Assessment of Quality in Graduate Education.* Washington, D.C.: American Council on Education, 1966.

CASSO, H. J., and ROMAN, G. D. (Eds.). *Chicanos in Higher Education.* Albuquerque: University of New Mexico Press, 1976.

CHICKERING, A. W. "Institutional Size and Student Development." Paper presented at the Council for the Advancement of Small Colleges Conference on Factors Affecting Student Development in College, 1965.

CHICKERING, A. W. *Education and Identity.* San Francisco: Jossey-Bass, 1969.

CIARDI, J. *Person to Person.* New Brunswick, N.J.: Rutgers University Press, 1964.

CLARK, B. R., and TROW, M. "The Campus as Viewed as a Culture." In H. T. Sprague (Ed.), *Research on College Students.* Boulder, Colo.: Western Interstate Commission for Higher Education; Berkeley, Calif.: Center for the Study of Higher Education, 1968.

CLARK, W. "Big and/or Little? Search Is on for Right Technology." *Smithsonian,* July 1976, pp. 43–48.

Clearinghouse for Community Based Free Standing Educational Institutions. "CBFSEI Newsletter." Washington, D.C., 1977.

CLINTON, W. J. "Center's New Survey Depicts Rapid Growth." *PSI Newsletter* [Washington, D.C.: Center for Personalized Instruction, Georgetown University], 1976, *4* (2), 1.

COHEN, A. M. *A Constant Variable.* San Francisco: Jossey-Bass, 1971.

CONANT, J. B. *The American High School Today: A 1st Report to Interested Citizens.* New York: McGraw-Hill, 1959.

121

References

CRITTENDEN, K. S., NORR, J. L., and LEBAILLY, R. K. "Size of University Classes and Teaching Evaluation." *Journal of Higher Education*, 1975, *4*, 461–470.

CROSS, K. P. *Beyond the Open Door: New Students to Higher Education.* San Francisco: Jossey-Bass, 1971.

CROSS, K. P. *Accent on Learning: Improving Instruction and Reshaping the Curriculum.* San Francisco: Jossey-Bass, 1976.

DE ZUTTER, P. "The Uses of Alliance." *American Education*, Aug. 1973, pp. 16–22.

DUBIN, R., and TRAVEGGIA, T. C. *The Teaching-Learning Paradox.* Eugene: Center for Advanced Study of Educational Administration, University of Oregon Press, 1968.

FELDMAN, K. A., and NEWCOMB, T. M. *The Impact of College on Students.* (2 vols.) San Francisco: Jossey-Bass, 1969.

FISKE, E. "Schools Like Doctors Being Charged with Malpractice." *New York Times*, March 9, 1977a, p. B6.

FISKE, E. "Colleges Hail Ruling in Tuition Refund Suit." *New York Times*, June 29, 1977b, p. B4.

Fund for the Improvement of Postsecondary Education. *Resources for Change.* (3 vols.) Washington, D.C.: U.S. Government Printing Office, 1975–1978.

GAFF, J. G. *The Cluster College.* San Francisco: Jossey-Bass, 1970.

GALLANT, J. A., and PROTHERO, J. W. "Weight Watching at the University: Consequences of Growth." *Science*, 1972, 175–180.

GITTELL, M., and DOLLAR, J. "Cultural Pluralism in Higher Education." *Social Policy*, November/December, 1974, pp. 38–45.

GREEN, B. A., JR. "Fifteen Reasons Not to Use the Keller Plan." In J. G. Sherman (Ed.), *Personalized Systems of Instruction: 41 Germinal Papers.* Menlo Park, Calif.: W.A. Benjamin, 1974.

GRUPE, F. "Cross Registration in the Associated Colleges of the St. Lawrence Valley." *The Acquainter Newsletter* [Birmingham: University of Alabama], April 1976, p. 3.

GUITIERREZ, G. *Final Report of the San Jose City College Women's*

References

Re-Entry Program. Unpublished report submitted to the Fund for the Improvement of Postsecondary Education, Washington, D.C., 1975.

HEIST, P., and BILORUSKY, J. "A Special Breed of Student." In J. G. Gaff (Ed.), *The Cluster College.* San Francisco: Jossey-Bass, 1970.

HILL, P. J. "The Federated Course Approach at Stony Brook." Unpublished memorandum. Stony Brook: State University of New York, 1976.

HOLMSTROM, E. I. "Low-Income Students: Do They Differ From 'Typical' Undergraduates?" *American Council on Education Research Report,* 1973, *8* (5).

"How Big: A Review of Literature on the Problems of Campus Size." Unpublished report. Los Angeles: Division of Institutional Research, California State College, 1970.

HOWE, F. *Seven Years Later: Women's Studies Programs in 1976: A Report of the National Advisory Council on Women's Educational Programs.* Washington, D.C.: National Advisory Council on Women's Educational Programs, 1977.

Institute for Services to Education. "Report on Predominantly Black Institutions." Washington, D.C.: Institute for Services to Education, 1973.

JENCKS, C., and RIESMAN, D. *The Academic Revolution.* New York: Doubleday, 1969.

KERR, C. *The Uses of the University.* New York: Harper & Row, 1963.

KERR, C. "Conservatism, Dynamism and the Changing University." In A. C. Eurich (Ed.), *Campus 1980: The Shape of the Future in American Higher Education.* New York: Delacorte Press, 1968.

KERSHAW, J. A. *The Very Small College.* New York: Ford Foundation, 1976.

LADD, D. R. "Achieving Change in Educational Policy in American Colleges and Universities." *Annals of the American Academy of Political and Social Science,* 1972, *404,* 207–216.

123

References

LIGUORI, R. A., and HARRIS, M. B. "Some Effects of a Personalized System of Instruction in Teaching College Mathematics." *Journal of Educational Research*, 1974, *68*, 62–67.

LOCKE, P. "WICHE Report on American Indian Higher Education." Boulder, Colo.: Western Interstate Commission on Higher Education, 1976.

MCKEACHIE, W., and BORDEN, E. "Size of Class Instruction as a Factor in the Enjoyment of Teaching." *Journal of Higher Education*, 1961, *32*, 339–343.

MAEROFF, G. "Berkeley Is Trying Informal Approach." *New York Times*, December 11, 1976, p. 56.

"Making It Count: A Report on a Project to Provide Better Financial Aid Information to Students." Princeton, N.J.: College Scholarship Service, College Entrance Examination Board, 1977.

Malcolm-King: Harlem College Extension. *Final Report on FIPSE Project.* Unpublished report submitted to the Fund for the Improvement of Postsecondary Education, Washington, D.C., 1975.

MANCUSO, J. "Legal Rights to Reasonable Rules, Fair Grades, and Quality Courses." In J. S. Stark (Ed.), *New Directions for Higher Education: Promoting Consumer Protection for Students,* no. 13. San Francisco: Jossey-Bass, 1976.

MEDSKER, L. L. *Breaking the Access Barriers: A Profile of Two-Year Colleges.* New York: McGraw-Hill, 1971.

MESKILL, V. "Weekend College." In D. W. Vermilye (Ed.), *Learner-Centered Reform: Current Issues in Higher Education 1975.* San Francisco: Jossey-Bass, 1975.

MUSCATINE, C. *The Muscatine Report.* Berkeley: University of California, 1966.

MUSCATINE, C. *Proposal for a Collegiate Seminar Program.* Berkeley: University of California, 1973.

MUSCATINE, C. "Annual Report on Strawberry Creek College." Berkeley: University of California, 1975.

National Center for Education Statistics. *Digest of Education Statistics 1971.* Washington, D.C.: U.S. Government Printing Office, 1971.

References

National Center for Education Statistics. *The Condition of Education.* Washington, D.C.: U.S. Government Printing Office, 1976.

National Institute of Education. *Youth Policy in Transition: A Report.* Washington, D.C.: National Institute of Education, 1976.

National Science Board. *Graduate Education: Perimeters for Public Policy.* National Science Foundation. Washington, D.C.: U.S. Government Printing Office, 1969.

NEWCOMB, T. "Student Peer-Group Influences." In N. Sanford (Ed.), *The American College.* New York: Wiley, 1962.

Office of Institutional Research. *Open Admissions at the City University of New York 1970–1975: An Evaluation.* New York: City University of New York, 1976.

PACE, C. R. *The Demise of Diversity.* Berkeley, Calif.: Carnegie Commission on Higher Education, 1974.

PACKWOOD, W. T. (Ed.). *College Personnel Services.* Springfield, Ill.: Thomas, 1977.

PATTERSON, F. "The Consortia: Interinstitutional Cooperation in American Higher Education." A draft report to the Ford Foundation, 1973.

PATTERSON, F. *Colleges in Consort: Institutional Cooperation Through Consortia.* San Francisco: Jossey-Bass, 1974.

PATTERSON, L. D. *Consortia in Higher Education.* Washington, D.C.: ERIC Clearinghouse, 1970.

PATTERSON, L. D. *Consortia in Higher Education.* Washington, D.C.: American Association for Higher Education, 1975.

PATTERSON, L. D. *Consortia in American Higher Education.* Washington, D.C.: ERIC Clearinghouse, 1977.

PETERSON, R. E., and BILORUSKY, J. *May 1970: The Campus Aftermath of Cambodia and Kent State.* New York: McGraw-Hill, 1971.

QUEHL, G. H. "Autonomy and Control in Voluntary Consortia." In D. W. Vermilye (Ed.), *The Expanded Campus: Current Issues in Higher Education 1972.* San Francisco: Jossey-Bass, 1972.

RAMIREZ, M., and CASTANEDA, A. *Cultural Democracy, Biocognitive Development and Education.* New York: Academic Press, 1974.

References

REED, B. "Collaborative Women's Studies." *Great Lakes Colleges Association Newsletter*, May 1978, pp. 4–6.

ROBIN, A. L. "Behavioral Instruction in the College Classroom." *Review of Educational Research*, 1976, *46* (3), 320–340.

ROOSE, K. D., and ANDERSON, C. J. *A Rating of Graduate Programs.* Washington, D.C.: American Council on Education, 1970.

RUSH, C. A. "The Cross Registration Program of the Pittsburgh Council on Higher Education." Unpublished doctoral dissertation, University of Pittsburgh, 1977.

SANFORD, N. *Where Colleges Fail: A Study of the Student as a Person.* San Francisco: Jossey-Bass, 1967.

SCHUMACHER, E. F. *Small Is Beautiful.* New York: Harper & Row, 1973.

SHER, J. P., and TOMPKINS, R. B. "Myths of Rural School and District Consolidation." *Educational Forum*, 1976, *41*, 94–107; 137–153.

SHERMAN, J. G. (Ed.). *Personalized Systems of Instruction: 41 Germinal Papers.* Menlo Park, Calif.: W. A. Benjamin, 1974.

SMITH, V. B. "More for Less: Higher Education's New Priority." In L. Wilson and D. Mills (Eds.), *Universal Higher Education: Costs and Benefits.* Washington, D.C.: American Council on Education, 1971.

SMITH, V. B. "Individualized Self-Paced Instruction." In R. S. Ruskin and S. S. Bono (Eds.), *Personalized Instruction in Higher Education.* Proceedings of the 1st National Conference. Washington, D.C.: Center for Personalized Instruction, Georgetown University, 1974.

STAKENAS, R. G. "Student-Faculty Contact and Attitude Change: Results of an Experimental Program for College Freshmen." In K. A. Feldman (Ed.), *College and Student: Selected Readings in the Social Psychology of Higher Education.* New York: Pergamon Press, 1972.

STANNARD, C. *Final Report on Binghamton/Broome Joint Degree Program.* Unpublished report submitted to the Fund for the Improvement of Postsecondary Education, Washington, D.C., 1977.

STARK, J. S. (Ed.). *New Directions for Higher Education: Promot-*

References

ing Consumer Protection for Students, no. 13. San Francisco: Jossey-Bass, 1976.

Staten Island Community College. *Proposal to Evaluate the People Center.* New York: Staten Island Community College, 1975.

STEGMAN, W. N. "A Study to Develop Living Area Activities Designed to Improve the Retention Ratio of Potential Student Dropouts." Final report. Washington, D.C.: U.S. Office of Education, 1969.

STEIN, H. D. "Evaluation Report on the Joint Faculty Junior Appointments Program of Five Colleges, Inc." Cleveland, Ohio: Case Western Reserve University, 1977.

STURNER, W. F. "The College Environment." In D. W. Vermilye (Ed.), *The Future in the Making: Current Issues in Higher Education 1973.* San Francisco: Jossey-Bass, 1973.

SUTHERLAND, G. "Is There an Optimum Size for a University?" *Minerva,* 1973, *2,* 53–78.

TOFT, R. *Final Report on Grand Valley College IV.* Unpublished report submitted to the Fund for the Improvement of Postsecondary Education, Washington, D.C., 1975.

TROMBLEY, W. "Research Challenges Freshmen: Experimental UC College Offers Series of Seminars." *Los Angeles Times,* Sept. 28, 1975, Pt. 2, pp. 1–4.

University of California, Irvine. "Prospectus." Irvine: University of California, 1976.

University of Maryland, Baltimore County. *Task Force Report for Middle States Accreditation Visit,* 1975.

WARREN, J. R. *Report on Academic Competencies Project.* Berkeley, Calif.: Educational Testing Service, 1977.

WUEST, F. "Colegio Cesar Chavez." *Project on Liberal Learning Newsletter* [Washington, D.C.: Association of American Colleges], 1976, *2* (2), 1.

127

Index

129

Index

Attrition rates in community colleges, 95
Atypical students, 91–106
Auto-tutorial instruction, 66, 71, 72

B

BALDRIDGE, J. V., 115, 120
Barat College, 75
BARKER, R. G., 16, 120
BAYER, A. E., 20, 120
Bensalem College, 52
Berkeley, Strawberry Creek College at, 58–64
BERNSTEIN, A. R., x, xviii, 120
Bicultural learning centers, 93
Bigger is better myths, 1–14
BILORUSKY, J., 21, 92, 123, 125
Black Hills State College, 105
Black students, 92, 93
BLACKBURN, R., 8, 27, 61, 120
Block scheduling, 84, 85
Bolivar, University of, 44
BORDEN, E., 124
Boredom and individualized instruction, 71
Boricua, Universidad, 93
BOWEN, F. M., 18, 30, 120
BOWEN, H. R., 120
BOWERS, W. J., 17, 18, 120
BOYLE, B. M., 120
BRENEMAN, E., 29, 120
Bridgeport, University of, 78
Broome Community College, 31, 42
Budgets: and expansion, 8; review committee participation, 17; slashing of, xii; supervision of, 14
Bureaucracy: and action/research, 115; and consortia, 30
BURN, N., 35, 120–121
BUSHNELL, R. A., 121

C

CAI, 66–73
Camposines Libres, Universidad de, 102
Capital costs, 11, 12
Career shopping, 8
Carnegie Commission on Higher Education, 47; on consortia, 29; on cooperative ventures, 43; and costs per student, 10, 11; and enrollment, 9; and size of institutions, 12
CARROLL, L., 65
CARTTER, A. M., 9, 121
CASSO, H. J., 106, 121
CASTANEDA, A., 102, 126
Ceilings on enrollments, 5
Central Harlem Association of Montessori Parents, 101
Central Pennsylvania Consortium, 44
Centralization of universities, 2, 3
Cesar Chavez Colegio, 93, 102, 103
Change and economic pressures, 107–118
Cheating and size of college, 17, 18
Checkpoints for consortia, 46, 47
Chicago, University of, 35
Chicano colleges, 101–103
Chicano students, 106
CHICKERING, A. W., x, 121
CIARDI, J., 1, 2, 121
Circuit riders, 38
Claremont Center, 28
CLARK, B. R., 117, 121
CLARK, W., 121
Clark College, 28
Class size, 19, 20; and communication, 22
Clearinghouse for Community Based Free Standing Educational Institutions (CBFSEI), 104
Climate of institution, 20–22
CLINTON, W. J., 121
Cluster colleges, 49–64; typical students in, 92

130

Index

Coffee shops on campus, 87
COHEN, A. M., 81, 121
Colegio Cesar Chavez, 93, 102–103
Colegio de la Tierra, 102
Collaborations, 27–47
Colleges in Consort, 47
Collegiate Seminar Program, 49
Communication, 22, 23
Community building, classes for, 88
Community centers, 86
Community colleges, 91–106; attrition rates in, 95; and career shopping, 8; comprehensiveness as goal of, 6; establishment of, 4; and nontraditional students, 94–96; and self-paced learning modules, 68
Complementary consortia, 42
Comprehensiveness, 5–10; and consortia, 30, 31, 40–43
Computer assisted instruction, 66–73
CONANT, J. B., 5, 6, 121
Concentration of universities, 2
Consortia, 28–47; and comprehensiveness, 40–43; for off-campus learning, 43–46; and specialization, 33–40
Consumer information, 73–78
Contracts: learning, 101; violations of, by institutions, 77, 78
Cooperative arrangements among colleges, 28–47
Core curriculum, 51
Costs per student, 10, 11
Council for Interinstitutional Leadership, 29
Counseling services, 78–83
Criteria for consortia, 28, 29
Critical mass in education, 9
CRITTENDEN, K. S., 19, 122
CROSS, K. P., 66–73, 94, 122
Cross-registration, 33, 40, 41
Curriculum: and communication, 22; complementary, 42; and costs per student, 10, 11

D

DE ZUTTER, P., 122
Degree program at Strawberry Creek College, 62, 63
Demographically typical students, 92
Demonstrations by students, 21
Denison College, 37
DePauw College, 37
Development of students, 16–18
Dickinson College, 44
Dining facilities, 22
Disadvantaged students and block scheduling, 84
Disaffection of students, x
Discrimination and size of institutions, 21, 22
Diseconomies of scale, 15–25
Dismissal of students, law suits involving, 77
Distribution requirements at Strawberry Creek College, 62
Diversity: of course offerings, xi; and electives, 8; options of, 27, 28
Dixon Doctrine, 77
DOLLAR, J., 95, 101, 122
Dormitory life, 22, 111
D-Q University, 102
Drug abuse, 7
DUBLIN, R., 19, 122
Due process in dismissal of students, 77

E

Earlham College, 37
Economic pressures and changes, 107–118
Economies of scale, 3, 10–14; and introductory lecture classes, 18
Economists and size of institutions, x
Educated person, determination of, 61, 62
Education Amendments of 1972, 3

131

Index

Educational prospectus, 74, 75
Educational psychologists, x
Efficiency and centralization, 2
Electives and specialization, 8
ELGIN, D. S., 121
Empire State College, 12
Enrollment: and aid programs, 13; ceilings on, 5; and comprehensiveness, 6; and critical mass, 9; magic figure for, 9: peril points in, 13
Environment of college, and student development, x
Ethnic clubs, 86
Evaluation of instruction, 19, 20
Examinations, 19
Expansion: and enervation, 2; and experimental education, 12; increasing options without, 27–47; limiting of, 5; and vitality, 14
Experimental education, 12
Extracurricular activities, 16, 17

F

Faculty: joint appointment of, 33–35; women in, 14
Familia, concept of, 102, 103
Federated courses, 54–56
Feeder institutions, 93
FELDMAN, K. A., 122, 127
Financial assistance, 76
Finger Lakes Center, 29, 44
Fiscal constraint, xii
FISKE, E., 78, 122
Five Colleges, Inc., 33, 34
Food services, 86, 87
Fordham University, 52, 99
Foreign studies, 32
4-1-4 calendar and cross-registration, 41
Franklin and Marshall College, 44
Fraternities, 86, 111
Free universities, 93

Freshman cluster, 54–60
Fund for the Improvement of Postsecondary Education, ix, 45; and adaptability, 23; and women's studies, 38
Funding of Strawberry Creek College, 63

G

GAFF, J., 50, 122
GALLANT, J. A., 10, 20, 122
GARDNER, J., 4
General education at Strawberry Creek College, 61, 62
Georgetown University, Center for Personalized Instruction at, 68
Gettysburg College, 44
GITTELL, M., 95, 101, 122
Graduate education: admissions committees of, 17; and enrollment, 9, 10
Grand Valley State Colleges system (Michigan), 71
Great Lakes Colleges Association, 30, 33, 37–39
GREEN, B., 73, 122
Group discussions, 63, 64
Group research projects, 88
Growth. *See* Expansion
GRUPE, F., 40, 122
GUITIERREZ, G., 84, 122–123
GUMP, P., 16, 120

H

Hamilton College, 32
Hampshire College, 33
Harlem College Extension, 93, 98
Harpur College of SUNY, 42
HARRIS, M. B., 73, 124
Haskell Indian Junior College, 97
Hebrew University, 32
HEIST, P., 92, 123

132

Index

Henderson State University, 42
HEW, ix; and *Youth Policy in Transition*, 6
High schools, size of, 5
HILL, P., 55, 56, 123
Hispanic International University, 102
HOLMSTROM, E. I., 95, 123
Hope College, 37
Hostels for students, 86
Hostos Community College, 99
HOWE, F., 38, 86, 123
HUTCHINS, R., 51

I

Identity of learning community, 110, 111
Indian Self-Determination Act, 97
Indian students, 96–98
Individualized instruction, 66–73
Inflation, effect of, 109, 110
Institute for American Indian Arts, 97
Institutional climate, 20–22
Instruction techniques and size of institutions, 18–20
Interaction between student and teacher, 72, 73
Interconstituency sports, 86
Internships, 31, 32, 43, 44
Interviews as admissions procedure, 100
Introductory lecture classes, 18
Irvine, University of California at, 74, 75, 85
Isolation and Great Lakes Colleges Association, 37

J

Jacinto Trevino, Universidad, 102
JENCKS, C., 92, 123

Joint faculty appointments, 33–35
Joint internship programs, 31, 32
Juarez-Lincoln University, 102
Judaic studies, 35, 36
Junior colleges. *See* Community colleges
Junior year abroad programs, 31, 32, 43, 44

K

Kalamazoo College, 37
Keller Graduate School of Management, 36, 37
Kenyon College, 37
KERR, C., xviii, 6, 7, 108, 118, 123
KERSHAW, J. A., 12, 123

L

LADD, D. R., 24, 123
Law suits against institutions, 77, 78
Learning community, identity of, 110, 111
Learning contracts, 101
Learning modes, 87, 88
Learning skills: acquisition of, 57; at Strawberry Creek College, 58–60; at University of Maryland at Baltimore County, 56, 57
LE BAILLY, R. K., 19, 122
LEE, E. C., 19, 30, 119, 120
Letters of recommendation, 17
LIGUORI, R. A., 73, 124
Lilly Foundation, 38
LOCKE, P., 97, 105, 124
Loyola University, 35

M

MC KEACHIE, W., 22, 124
MAEROFF, G., 124

133

Index

Malcolm-King College, 93, 96, 98–101, 124
Management courses, 36
MANCUSO, J. H., 77, 124
Manhattan College, 32
Maryland, University of, at Baltimore County, 54–60
Marymount Manhattan College, 99
Mass production, 3, 4
Massachusetts, University of, 33, 35
Master learner, 55, 56
MEDSKER, L. L., 6, 124
Memos from administration, 22, 23
MESKILL, V., 124
Michigan, University of, Residential College at, 52
Minority students, 91–106
Monteith College, 52
Morehouse College, 28
Morris Brown College, 28
Mt. Angel College, 102
Mt. Holyoke College, 33
Mount St. Vincent, College of, 99
Multiple-choice examinations, 19, 20
Multiunit universities, 2, 3
Mundelein College, 35
MUSCATINE, C., 59, 60, 61, 63, 124
Mysore, University of, 44
Myths of bigger is better, 1–14

N

National Science Board, 9
Navajo Community College, 97, 98
Navajo tribe, 97
New York University, 32
NEWCOMB, T., 17, 111, 122, 125
Newspapers, working on, 17
Noninstructional student personnel services, 109
Nontraditional academic programs, x
Nontraditional students, 91–106
NORR, J. L., 19, 122

Northeast Nebraska Technical Community College, 97
Northwestern University, 35

O

Oberlin College, 37
Objective examinations, 19
Occupational programs in community colleges, 8
Off-campus learning, consortia for, 43–46
Oglala Sioux Community College, 93, 98, 105
Ohio Wesleyan University, 37
Old Sturbridge Village, 46
Older students, xi
Open admissions, 94, 95
Options and expansion, 27–47
Oregon Zoological Research Center, 45
Outcome and size of institutions, x
Overcrowding, 7
Overspecialization at Strawberry Creek College, 61, 62

P

PACKWOOD, W. T., 109, 125
PAGE, C. R., 125
Participation of students, 18
PATTERSON, F., 28, 47, 125
PATTERSON, L. D., 28, 29, 31, 40, 41, 44, 46, 125
Peer groups, learning from, 111
Personalized system of instruction (PSI), 66–73
PETERSON, R. E., 21, 125
Pittsburgh Council on Higher Education, 40
Planning: and costs, 11, 12; and 1202 commissions, 3

Index

Index

Spelman College, 28
Spertus College, of Judaica, 35, 36
Stability, 23, 24
STAKENAS, R. G., 126
Standing Rock Community College, 98
Stanford University, 32
STANNARD, C., 42, 43, 126–127
STARK, J. S., 76, 127
Staten Island Community College, 80
Status quo, preservation of, 109
STEGMAN, W. N., 127
STEIN, H. D., 127
Stony Brook (SUNY), 54–56
Strawberry Creek College, 49, 50, 56–64
Strikes by students, 21
Structural organization, 83–85; and action/research, 114–117
Student body president, 17
Student government, 16, 17
Student personnel services, 78–83
Sturbridge Village, 46
STURNER, W. F., 127
Support services, 78–83; and action/research, 116
SUTHERLAND, G., 9, 127

T

Teaching modes, 87, 88
Team teaching, 84, 85
Technical schools, 3
Tenure in joint programs, 34
Tests, 19
Toft, R., 71, 127
Tompkins, R. B., 6, 126
Trade and technical schools, 3
Traveggia, T. C., 19, 122
Trombley, W., 127
Trow, M., 117, 121
Tussman, J., 51
Tussman College, 51
1202 commissions, 3

Two-year colleges. *See* Community colleges

U

Undergraduate, defined, 91
Union of Independent Colleges of Art, 47
Universidad Boricua, 93, 98, 99–103
Universidad de Camposines Libres, 102
Universidad Jacinto Trevino, 102
Urban semester program, 44
Uses of the University, The, 6, 7

V

Values, development of, 17, 18
Vassar College, 32
Vermont Community College, 12
Very Small College, The, 12
Visiting scholar, 38
Vitality, 23–25
Vocational programs, 3; and comprehensiveness, 8; in consortia, 42

W

Wabash College, 37
Warren, J. R., 8, 127
Washington, University of, 85
Washington summer internship program, 32
Wayne University, Monteith College at, 52
Weekend colleges, 83, 84
Welfare system, 81
Wellesley College, 32
West Germany and student law suits, 77
Whitman College, 45
Wilson College, 44
Working adult students, xi

Index

Women: centers for, 86; consortia study program on, 30, 31; in faculty, 140; and joint degree in women's studies, 38, 39
Wooster College, 37
Worcester Art Museum, 46
Worcester Consortium for Higher Education, 45
Worcester County Horticultural Society, 46
Writing labs, 85

Writing skills, development of, 19, 20
Written examinations, 19
Wuest, F., 102, 127

Y

Year abroad programs, 31, 32, 43, 44
Youth Policy in Transition, 6